Teacher Burnout
and What to do About it

Teacher Burnout
and What to do About it

Stephen Truch, PhD
Academic Therapy Publications
Novato, California

Copyright © 1980, by Academic Therapy Publications, Inc. All rights reserved. Printed in the United States of America. No part of this publication may be rproduced, stored in a retrieval system, or transmitted, in any form or by any means, electronic, mechanical photocopying, recording, or otherwise, without the prior written permission of the publisher.

Academic Therapy Publications
20 Commercial Boulevard
Novato, California 94947

Books, tests, and materials for and about the learning disabled
International Standard Book Number: 0-87879-242-2

9 8 7 6 5 4 3 2 1 0
0 9 8 7 6 5 4 3 2 1

For Alita, Kama and Jackie.

Contents

Acknowledgements..xi

CHAPTER ONE
Teachers—An Endangered Species?........................... 1

CHAPTER TWO
A Brief History..13

CHAPTER THREE
Teaching Now—A Self-Destruct Career.......................19

CHAPTER FOUR
You Say Johnny Can't Read?....................................29

CHAPTER FIVE
Teacher Stress: Basic Theory....................................39

CHAPTER SIX
The Concept of Stress..47

CHAPTER SEVEN
The R.E.A.D. Program for Managing Personal Stressors..............57

CHAPTER EIGHT
Managing Stress in Schools.....................................73

CHAPTER NINE
Managing Classroom Stressors 81

Appendix A 97
    Life Stress Scales I & II 99
    Student Stress Scale 101
    Stress Profile for Teachers 103
    "Hurry Sickness" Index 107

Appendix B 109
    Coping Scale 111
    The "Wellness Behavior" Test 113

Appendix C 115
    An Outside In Procedure for Relaxing 117

Appendix D 123
    An Outside In Procedure for Teaching Children to Relax 125

References 133

About the Author 139

Acknowledgements

I would like to express my thanks to several people. First, to Scott Lowe, for his editorial craftsmanship and expertise in providing direction and polish to this work. Also, to John Arena and the other good people at Academic Therapy for their support and encouragement throughout. I would also like to thank Faye McCuskee and the "Sundre crew" for typing the manuscript.

As with any major undertaking, a large sacrifice of time is necessary. I would therefore like to give my major thank you to my family for their patience, understanding, and support.

Chapter One

Teachers— An Endangered Species?

Teachers are leaving their profession at an accelerated pace.

In a recent poll, one-third of the teachers contacted said they would not go back to teaching if they had the chance to do it again. Only 60 percent of those polled said they plan to teach until retirement. As yet another indicator of teacher dropout, the number of teachers with twenty years or more experience has dropped by half in the last fifteen years.[1]

It seems that younger teachers are leaving within the first five years of teaching (in most cases because they still have a chance to be retrained in another field) and older teachers are retiring earlier.[2]

More medical insurance claims are being made by teachers than from other professions. In England, the deaths of male teachers approaching retirement has doubled in the last ten years. The number of teachers qualifying for a breakdown pension has tripled.[3] Results of a recent study indicate the life expectancy of a teacher is four years lower than the national average.[4]

Some surveys indicate 90 percent of all teachers feel some stress and 95 percent indicate the need for stress management courses.[5] Others estimate that teaching may be the third most stressful occupation on earth, following air traffic controllers and surgeons.

Why are so many teachers unhappy? Why are they leaving their careers even when jobs are scarce and salaries high?

Alienation, isolation, a sense of powerlessness, and self-estrangement help to create a climate of great dissatisfaction and frustration with teaching. Fortunately, this is not so with all teachers, but there is no doubt that teaching is just not what it was twenty years ago.

Declining enrollments, role conflicts, time pressures, inadequate administrative support, lack of self-control in children, public pressures (often unrealistic and political in origin), and an attitude that education must be "all things to all people" have greatly increased teacher stress. Teachers, too, are trapped in the twentieth century malaise of rapidly changing conditions.

Teacher morale has been the subject of various briefs, papers, presentations, and government commissions on declining enrollments. Declining enrollments have contributed to teacher stress by creating job uncertainty and restricting both teacher mobility and promotions.

An example of administrative nonsupport creating extreme job uncertainty occurred when a lottery draw was made to establish the seniority rankings of over 500 teachers. Over half of them were terminated because of declining enrollments. One teacher, who survived the lottery and therefore had work for awhile said, "It's been such a strain waiting to find out, that to get some feeling of security for at least a year or two is such a relief. I'm stunned. It's a hard thing to realize I may have made the wrong choice in becoming a teacher." Another teacher, not so fortunate, said, "It's an incredible feeling. I couldn't believe it when they told me. . . . It's one thing to be unemployed, another to know that you're going to be."[6]

One Example

Teachers are trapped and squeezed by pressures both sometimes beyond their control and sometimes created by themselves. The web is always complex, as the following personal history illustrates.[7]

> I had no trouble getting a job close to home and I had my choice of two or three. That is not to say that the pay was good or that the working conditions were ideal. My first principal was a cruel man who ran the school on a policy of distrust. He was rude, tyrannical and dictatorial. I was able to survive and grow into my job while two of the new teachers who started with me were driven out of the profession by a combination of tough kids and a hard principal.
>
> In the midsixties I moved to a small town. I met a handful of dedicated people who broke new ground in every possible area of teaching. The kids were good and wanted to do well and I still look back on this period as crucial to my own professional development. That little staff was the most superior, hard working group I have ever met. Our kids walked off with a disproportionate number of honors and scholarships. They were proud of their records and so were we.
>
> In 1966 the School Board decided to close the small school and

I took a job in another town. I took a year or so to adjust to the new job and staff but found a good deal to admire there. A tradition of excellence was already established in this school and I found it to my liking. I grew very close to all of the staff over the ten years I was there and when I left it was a gut wrenching event in my life.

During those years my wife tried to find a job to help out with the finances. There never was enough money to keep us out of debt and she had a strong desire to establish herself in a career of her own. The problem was that she had a medical condition which caused her to lose a lot of time from work. Still, she was quite successful as a real estate saleswoman.

A number of events culminated in opening our own company. I had begun to look for a new career and if my wife could keep up the success she had had, we would soon have a thriving business. I did not care for real estate but the pressure of teaching had reached an uncomfortable level and getting out seemed attractive. Our company lasted the first year quite well and looked hopeful going into the second. I was making plans to quit teaching by the end of the year. However, once again my wife became ill. We were warned that she would have to find a solution to her allergies or face serious chronic illness.

Investigation proved that the West was a suitable location and since her family was there, the decision to move was logical. However, it was necessary to close out the business; it was a financial disaster. The only stable element in our financial life was my teaching job and it was in the East while my family moved West. Eventually, I had to resign and move to the West as well. I resented being forced to make that move but there was no alternative. I resigned my position and began looking for a job out West.

I was fortunate to find one quickly, just an hour's drive from where we were living. The new system was totally different from the system I had left and I felt very unhappy with my lot in life. The teaching staff was lazy, poorly trained, and lacked any of the professional interests I was accustomed to. The students were disruptive and a state of open hostility existed between them and the staff when I arrived. The financial cost of the move, the loss of my friends, my dissatisfaction with the unprofessional attitude of the new staff members, and the numerous long teaching days proved almost too much for me. I began to have chest pains, stomach upset and general tension attacks. I reached the verge of a nervous breakdown and only managed to survive because of the coming of the summer break.

In the fall I was much improved, and the main reason for that was a renewed interest in a career outside of teaching. With the assurance that I could find a job outside of teaching if I wanted it, I found teaching in the new system bearable. I received training over the summer in a field of business which may yet offer me a full time career, and is offering a part time occupation now. To know that I can get out of teaching if the pressure becomes too great has been my lifeline this past year. What I have discovered about myself, however, is that I am a creative and successful teacher and that teaching is my first choice of profession. I would rather teach than do anything else, but there is a breaking point to my health now and I will have to be careful not to cross that point.

This man's teaching career spans some fifteen years. In that time, he has become an excellent teacher. In his own life he has experienced numerous job and personal stressors. He is still coping now—and still in the classroom. His students are the beneficiaries of his tenacity because he is indeed a creative teacher. But how long can he last? What support is he receiving to help ensure that he remains in the classroom? In fact, he is not receiving any support other than that which he has sought out for himself. His is a classic case where economic and other twentieth century pressures have produced psychosomatic illness and marked unhappiness. Worse, he doesn't want anyone to know about it, least of all his supervisors.

This teacher is having a tough time remaining in his chosen profession. Many other good teachers are already on the verge of exiting. Many others have already left. Of those who do, the full reasons they have left teaching are unknown because accurate statistics have not been kept. But we do know that teachers all over North America are experiencing great stress and many are burning out completely.

Teacher Burnout

Some authorities consider teacher burnout "the biggest problem in education today."[8] Burnout is physical, emotional and attitudinal exhaustion:[9]

> The symptoms include being tired all of the time, sleeplessness, depression, and being physically run down. Teachers experiencing burnout often have minor physical maladies such as frequent colds, headaches, dizziness, or diarrhea. If unchecked, these ailments may turn into ulcers, colitis or asthma or they may cause loss of appetite and loss of sexual interest.
>
> Teachers who feel physically unwell soon find themselves depressed by their symptoms. It's difficult to play kickball with the kids when you are tired and slightly dizzy. It's difficult to be excited about a topic you are teaching when you are uncomfortable and out of sorts all the time. Teachers report that their self-concept drops to

a new low as they question the meaning of teaching. What's it all for, they ask. Why am I doing this? They see themselves becoming less effective with children and colleagues. "I have nothing to offer anymore," one teacher explained, "I hate coming to work. I am intolerant of childish behavior and I feel guilty collecting my salary. I feel as if I am a robot."

First things hurt in body and mind; then they actually start to fall apart at school. The teacher feels guilty, incompetent as an educator and finally inadequate as a person. This of course, affects personal relationships. If unchecked, burnout can result in total emotional breakdown.

Researchers have shown that responsibility for people always causes more stress than responsibility for things, so people involved in teaching, counseling, psychology, and all of the major health professions are particularly susceptible to this kind of occupational stress. Burnout tends to occur most frequently among the helping or people professions. The warning signs of burnout include physical signs like back pain, headaches, stomach pain, ulcers, exhaustion, sleeplessness, inability to shake colds; the emotional, psychological and behavioral signs of burnout include depression, discontent, detachment, dehumanization or robot-like behavior, negativity or cynicism, angry outbursts, self-abasement, rigidity, suspiciousness, silence and withdrawal, the attitude of just putting in time, making more mistakes on the job, leaving the job, low morale, and of course absenteeism.

The Battered Teacher

As if the pressure of the teaching job were not enough, many teachers face another great threat—physical abuse. The National Education Association (NEA) indicates that classroom stress is increasing at an alarming rate. Assaults are up 77 percent since 1972. In 1978 for example, 54,000 NEA members were physically attacked by students. In 1979 this had increased to 70,000. In 1978, 144,000 members had their personal property maliciously damaged. In 1979 this changed to 250,000 (1 in 8). In the same year, 500,000 (1 in 4) had personal property stolen.

More than 3,000 of the teachers who were attacked required emergency treatment in a hospital, more than 9,000 required attention in a clinic or doctor's room, and about 10,000 had to miss one or more days of school as a consequence.[10]

These grim statistics are accompanied by grim testimonies. Here is one documented story:[11]

> John S., a 41-year-old teacher, entered the sound and control booth of an inner city high school auditorium. As he closed the door, he

confronted two male students who had been cutting the power lines and smashing electrical equipment. One of the students fled; the other began beating Mr. S. with his fists. When the student who had fled returned he held John S. while the other grabbed a chair and began battering the teacher's head and shoulders. Mr. S.'s screams were unheard. The battering continued and John S. finally lost consciousness.

The author of this article, Dr. Alfred M. Bloch, has treated hundreds of battered teachers. They all suffer symptoms from either physical trauma or prolonged psychic stress to the extent that they can no longer return to teaching. All are on disability allowances as a result of their job harassment. Dr. Bloch describes the symptoms of the battered teacher as follows:[12]

> Many of the psychological symptoms of these teachers were similar to those of people who have suffered from combat neurosis and of survivors of war disasters (e.g., emotional tension, anxiety, insecurity, nightmares, excessive startle response, phobias, cognitive impairment, blurred vision, dizziness, fatigue, and irritability). Their physical symptoms, also similar to those of combat neurosis, ranged from headaches and skin disorders to peptic ulcers, hypertension, and respiratory problems.
>
> The teachers who have presented symptoms comparable to combat neurosis are the battered teachers of this report. Ironically, during interviews, many referred to their schools as battle zones.

There are other examples of "life in the combat zones" provided by Dr. Bloch. One teacher, Mr. K., caught a student stealing school equipment. The student drew a knife and threatened to kill him. When the matter was reported to the administration, the student was given a three-day suspension. When he returned to school, he continued his threats to murder Mr. K.:[13]

> A few weeks later, Mr. K. was surprised to find a door to the auditorium unlocked after school hours. As he opened the door, a metal chair and desk came crashing down from the balcony and missed him by inches. An investigation revealed that a booby trap had been set to be activated when that door opened.

Despite many requests for a transfer to another school, Mr. K. was not granted it. He is now unable to function in many capacities, continues to suffer symptoms of stress (nightmares, insomnia, depression) and is unable to teach effectively.

A female high school teacher, Ms. R., taught school successfully in

North Carolina for six years. While there, a student once threatened to "cut up her face." She was able to escape. Her principal handled the situation well enough that Ms. R. returned next day to the classroom with no apparent psychological damage.

The situation changed dramatically when she started teaching in a Los Angeles inner city school. The classroom was designed for 22 students but she had 30 to start. By the end of September, it was 56. Many were problem students.

She was threatened and harassed. This time when she reported it to the administration she was given no support. She became anxious and depressed.

Two months later, as she was passing out report cards, a group of female students became angry about their grades and set her hair on fire. Some other students put it out. When she reported the incident to the principal, she was criticized for not maintaining discipline. She was also told not to discuss the assault with other teachers. Ms. R. became agitated, anxious and more depressed. She was unable to return to teaching. Later, she was hospitalized after a suicide attempt.

Another high school teacher, Mr. F., was popular among students in another inner city school. One hot summer afternoon, he took his class outside to sit in the shade. Three males, none of whom were students in the school, approached the group. Mr. F. asked if he could help. Without replying, the three grabbed him, then kicked and beat him until he lost consciousness. He was treated for lacerations. He lost some teeth. Yet he was advised by his principal to return to school the next day "to show the students that violence had not won."[14] Since the incident, he has developed anxiety, nightmares and paranoia. He has not left teaching, but is looking for an alternative career.

In addition to outright battering, many students learn to play "fear games" with teachers, particularly novice teachers, substitutes, and student teachers. Some psychologists have studied the intricacies of these sophisticated "games," the object of which is not so much to terrorize as it is to shift the balance of classroom power into the hands of the students.[15] The students use body language, eye contact, and verbal games to intimidate. Expert at these games, they employ a variety of moves to make teachers fearful. The ultimate loser in this game is the student, of course, but the whole process is doomed to create educational bankruptcy. As one writer points out:[16]

> An interesting irony can be found here. Schools, which cater to individuals in their most violence-prone years, are the only institutions in our society other than prisons and mental institutions which require involuntary participation, and their staffs are least prepared for violence.

Caution—Teaching is Dangerous to Your Health

Even in a relatively safe school, the effects of stress can create serious problems for teachers. Symptoms which eventually may result in burnout manifest in basic patterns. Each pattern represents a typical reaction to stress.[17]

The Emotional Pattern

These symptoms include depression, irritability, anxiety, yelling, blaming others for the source of problems, excessive worrying, nightmares, feelings of unreality, apathy, urges to cry or run and hide, nervousness, emotional tension, and nervous or inappropriate laughter.

The Behavioral Pattern

These reactions include increased smoking, alcohol, and drug use or addiction, increased proneness to accidents, impulsive behavior, inability to concentrate, increased use of prescription medicines and over-the-counter medicines, such as aspirins, diet drugs, pain relievers, tranquilizers, and amphetamines.

Physiological Patterns

The physiological effects of stress are widespread. The reason for this is that they are mediated by all portions of the nervous system. For example, the cardiovascular system may be affected. Cardiovascular symptoms of stress include high blood pressure, rapid heart beat, and heart diseases. The human heart is a four-chambered organ. Each chamber must contract in the proper sequence or rhythm.

When the rhythm is disturbed, then the person suffers from what is called cardiac arhythmia. One form observed in stressful individuals is premature ventricular contraction, in which one of the chambers opens and closes in an incorrect sequence producing inefficient pumping of the heart. Another arhythmia is called atrial fibrillation. The symptoms are a very rapid heart beat from one area of the heart but insufficient blood pumped out at each beat.

Another cardiovascular effect is vascular headaches—the best known of which are migraines. These pains arise from unusual activity in one or more of the arterial systems surrounding the brain. In the case of migraines, the pain comes from an unusually strong and rapid dilation of blood vessels resulting in pain synchronous with the heart beat. It is commonly reported that people predisposed to such headaches will often show an increase in their frequency and severity when they are in a state of heightened stress.

Other stress symptoms of a physiological nature are mediated by the voluntary muscles. Common complaints include muscle contractions and tension headaches or tension in the muscles of the neck and shoulders. Others report tightness or tension in the muscles of the chest, which they may experience as difficulty breathing or a feeling of great weight on the chest. Other muscles in other parts of the body may also be involved. Chronic pain and tightness in the legs, arms, and buttocks as well as abdominal pain are frequently reported by people caught in a vicious stress cycle.

Another organ system commonly involved in stress is the gastrointestinal system. It's been known for many years that certain types of ulcers are caused by stress and relieved by relaxation. Other gastrointestinal symptoms include spastic colitis, which is a spasmodic contraction of the smooth muscles in the area of the large intestine. This condition is extremely painful and may also interfere with digestion and elimination. Diarrhea is a stress symptom as is nausea. Functional constipation may also be related to the presence of stressors in a person's environment. The respiratory system can be affected too. Reactions to stress which manifest in this pattern include allergies such as hay fever, and skin problems such as eczema and psoriasis.

Finally, it has become increasingly clear that stress can produce profound effects on sexual functioning in individuals. One of the most telling symptoms of having been in a state of stress for a long time is the loss of any kind of desire for sexual activity. After a prolonged period of stress a person may become utterly sexually impotent.

Prevalence of Teacher Stress

To what extent do teachers display these patterns of stress? A four district survey of 75 teachers in San Diego revealed the following:[18] Many of the teachers (77 percent) reported physical signs of stress as present much of the time. Of the symptoms reported, 45 percent said they experienced stiff necks, 60 percent fatigue, 50 percent worry and 34 percent reported depression. All these symptoms were reported as occurring much of the time. An informal survey conducted by myself in a small rural district in Canada confirmed the same pattern. Obviously, no one is immune!

Another study, conducted in England, involved a random sample of over 300 teachers in large schools from urban centers.[19] Eighty percent completed the questionnaire. Teachers were asked to rate their responses to over fifty possible sources of teacher stress. The replies were quite revealing. About 20 percent of the teachers sampled rated teaching as either very stressful or extremely stressful. Furthermore, these ratings were not dependent on sex, qualifications, age, length of teaching experience, or position held in the school. This in itself is rather surprising and indicates the pervasive nature of the stress problem. It seems that, as another British researcher concludes, "Severe stress is being experienced by more teachers."[20]

The Cost of Teacher Stress

It is impossible to put a price tag on human misery. For example, how prevalent is the incidence of heart attack and ulcers in teachers and what does it cost the public? We can't answer either of those questions because there is precious little in the way of research on teacher burnout to provide a solid base. Do principals experience more stress than teachers? Again, we don't know but we might speculate that a principal is much like a foreman. He or she is caught in a "man in the middle" position between upper management and workers. Foremen have more ulcers as a consequence, but we don't know yet about principals.

Whenever there are conflicting role demands, a situation in which teachers and administrators often find themselves, then there is increased stress. This is so because of the "double bind" created when a person is forced to make a choice between two unpleasant alternatives. This can lead to psychosomatic illness, deterioration in work performance and productivity, less tolerance of others and, of course, increased absenteeism and deteriorating interpersonal relations. Teaching may involve over 1,200 interpersonal interactions in a single day! How can we expect maximum performance from an individual with that kind of emotional demand? And how can we calculate the loss to a child's personal growth because of it?

If we take just one aspect of teacher stress, namely absenteeism, then we might begin to get some idea of the direct cost. What is the rate of teacher absenteeism due to stress? In one Midwest survey, 35 percent of the teachers polled admitted that they called in ill occasionally because of fatigue or nervous tension. Seven percent said they were receiving psychiatric help, a fact they did not wish their employers to know, of course. The figures are much higher in other parts of the country. In San Diego, a recent survey indicated 90 percent of the educators there reported stress was often a cause for sick leave.[21] Teacher absenteeism has doubled in the last sixteen years in some parts of the country. The absentee rate is growing by 5 percent a year in Pennsylvania (higher than all other major industries) with that school district spending $27 million for substitutes every year!

Teachers, administrators, school boards, and the general public must work together to combat the problem. There are things that can be done and skills that can be learned and applied both to the school system and in the classroom. Some practical suggestions along these lines are presented in the latter part of this book.

However, the problem must be clearly understood in the broader context of society as a whole. The role of formal education is crucial in any industrialized nation. We need to discuss that role, to discuss and analyze the teaching profession itself, where it has come from and where it is going.

Although the coping skills are important in themselves, we must attempt to analyze what I consider to be deeper reasons why the teacher burnout problem is reaching what some already consider epidemic proportions.

Chapter Two

A Brief History

To appreciate teacher stress and burnout in contemporary society requires some understanding of the history of education on this continent. In North America, education has been, and still is, the people's servant. And the people are basically pragmatic. From early times, the public had rigid control over what should be taught, who should teach it, and what that teacher should say and think. Although there is much more freedom now, this is still largely true. Teachers are still expected to be solid middle-class citizens doing nothing more than what their communities expect of them.

What is taught in schools is determined by the state. What the state determines should be taught is based upon the political climate of the times. The present emphasis is to go "back to the basics," and the curricula attempt to reflect this. In some cases, teachers do have a say as to what is taught, particularly when they are allowed to sit on curriculum committees, but by and large, education is out of their hands.

Why is this so? No other profession is monitored as closely by the public. To get a better grasp of the situation, we must take a brief excursion into the history of teaching in North America. Teachers need to understand their roots on this continent in order to achieve some perspective and reflect on the direction the future must take.

What's Happened to Teacher?

In his book, *What's Happened To Teacher?*, Myron Brenton devotes a full chapter to the sad history of teaching.[1] That chapter forms the substance for this section. By way of summary, Brenton states:[2]

> His is a sorry history in many respects and not simply because of the way in which teachers were treated—the denial of rights which they endured, the servile manner in which they were expected to behave, the ludicrous wages they received, the political repression and other controls that were placed on them. It almost seems as though a deliberate attempt were being made on the part of the larger society to create a second-rate profession. Such a conspiratorial view stretches the point: The treatment accorded teachers simply reflects the fact that public school education did not, to put it mildly, occupy a very exalted place in the esteem of the nation. The frontier was nothing if not anti-intellectual. To be sure, the status of teachers varied from region to region and from period to period, as differing philosophical, religious, political, and economic forces played upon the concept of respect and recognition in their local communities. On the whole though, even when the hard fight to create a fully public school system was won after the Civil War, in many respects the teachers' place in society was little better than wretched.

In the beginning then, teachers occupied an extremely lowly, servile position. Religious instruction was the basis for Colonial "learning." In New England in the 1600s, towns of fifty families or more had to provide an elementary teacher, and towns of a hundred or more were required to establish a Latin grammar school for secondary instruction. Anyone who could afford to pay did so. There was, of course, no tax base for education at that time. Teachers were often drunkards, sadists, and swindlers. Many runaway servants became teachers and many of those ran away again from that.

Public and universal education was not implemented until the nineteenth century. Prior to that time, teaching was a part-time occupation. Many teachers were also clergymen. As a result, teachers often carried out semireligious duties, such as furnishing water for baptisms as well as bread and wine for communion, and digging graves.

School equipment was virtually nonexistent, student attendance irregular, the curriculum limited, and wages abysmal. Teachers were also boarded out on a weekly basis to local families to help stretch budgets. In those days, the teacher turnover rate was even more dismal than at present—around 40 percent.

The same conditions prevailed in terms of curriculum and materials in the eighteenth century, but the moral character of teachers was the primary focus. Teachers were often forced to sign elaborate oaths regarding their zeal for the Christian religion, their loyalty to the government, and their conformity to the doctrines of whatever church organization they were serving. But there was also an effort to provide instruction that would prepare an individual for life in the workaday world. Courses in bookkeeping and other subjects that could be applied directly in business and commerce were taught. None of this however, was in the hands of teachers themselves. They were still, after 200 years, simply doing what they were told.

The nineteenth century was a period of great progress. Public and compulsory education were established, in large part due to the efforts of Horace Mann, Henry Barnard, and others of like mind. New and better schools were built and the curriculum improved. Teachers began to form associations and schedule days for the discussion of the professional issues of the time, such as:[3]

> Is it better for teachers to board around? Should the teachers encourage pupils to chew tobacco? Should teachers open their schools in the morning by reading a portion of the Scripture? Should the door be closed against pupils who are not present at nine o'clock in the morning? Should the rod be used in school? Should the wages of females be equal to those of male teachers?

Educators had more than their share of difficulties. Farmers fought compulsory schooling. (Even today, students in rural areas often miss weeks of school at harvest time.) Students attended school on Saturdays, an ordeal we can hardly appreciate today. By Saturday, however, it had become dangerous to teach. "In 1872 in Ballard County, Kentucky's school commissioner protested the practice of people going 'to the school house to whip or insult a teacher.' His advice: 'If anyone desires to whip a teacher, let him wait until Saturday!'"[4]

To keep their jobs, teachers were forced to submit to annual exams conducted by laymen ignorant of teaching. Their queries and requirements were usually utterly unrelated to teaching itself. The rate of pay of male teachers was about half that of any skilled tradesman of the time. Female teachers had an even more difficult time of it, their rate being one-third or perhaps one-half of their male counterparts. In many cases, they made less than the janitors. Translated into dollars, female teachers in Boston in 1867 were receiving $2.50 a week. At the same time, cooks in Boston were receiving $3.00 weekly.

Well educated persons were hardly attracted to teaching. Turnover was very high, with many teachers serving only a seven-month term. Many handicapped persons became teachers. As one report stated, "... anyone can teach, especially if he happen to have been so unfortunate as to lose a limb, become blind in one eye, or in some way has become unfit for anything except a teacher. I know of no other business which has seemed to be so dependent on a bodily infirmity."[5]

Another major nineteenth century development was the shift to the predominance of women in teaching. Industrialization and urbanization drew many men away from teaching. The pay was better in industrial jobs, and increasingly, teaching was considered to be something that women did:[6]

> When, during the mid-1800's, a group of male teachers grumbled about the lack of esteem in which they were held by the community, famed suffragette Susan B. Anthony told them, "It seems to me that you fail to comprehend the cause of the disrespect of which you complain. Do you not see that so long as society says that woman has not brains enough to be a doctor, lawyer or minister, but has plenty to be a teacher, every one of you who condescends to teach tacitly admits before Israel and the sun that he has no more brains than a woman?"

Teachers were in bondage personally, socially, and economically. They were told how to dress, how and when to court, and for whom and how to vote. After five years teachers could expect a twenty-five cent raise, subject to Board approval. Under these most strenuous conditions, they were expected to save money for retirement "so as not to become a burden to society in their twilight years."[7]

That brings us back to the twentieth century, the Age of Stress. In the early 1900s, teachers were still being treated as wards of the state. The *Columbus Dispatch* in 1929 stated, "Teachers should know that it is part of American educational tradition that a teacher should have little or no freedom. She is born to be suppressed and harassed by a system of supervision designed to keep her docile."[8]

Teachers had to sign contracts promising not to get married, engaged, or even to fall in love. They also promised not to dance, to dress modestly, to sleep eight hours nightly, to actively participate in numerous church activities, and not to go out at night. Bobbed hair and makeup were seen as sinful. The fact that teaching was primarily an occupation for females allowed greater control in enforcing the image of morality and purity teachers were expected to represent.

The same attitudes prevail even today in the public mind, though not to the oppressive extent once displayed. In the last twenty years in particular, there have been tremendous advances in professionalism, personal freedom, and wages for teachers. Many still complain bitterly, but judging from the past three hundred years, teachers have come a long way.

This brief excursion into the past should provide a firmer and broader perspective on current conditions. If a 25 percent turnover rate seems high now, it is an improvement, not a decline from just 150 years ago. (Some school districts today, however, still have turnover rates of 40 percent or more). That is not to say I consider the problem of burnout any less serious. On the contrary, if teaching is ever to attain the status it deserves and burnout to burn out, it cannot come from being content over the present situation. There are extremely serious problems with teaching as a career profession which must be attended to. We will turn our attention now to some of these problems.

Chapter Three

Teaching Now—
A Self-Destruct Career

Everything about teachers in contemporary society is average. The average teacher is the average North American. Income is now about average for teachers. When asked to rank their own social status, teachers see themselves as "about average"—and indeed they are. Teachers by and large are caught in the comfortable middle-class rut.

Three Types of Teachers

In my experience with teachers, I find they fit in one of three groups. (On the average, that is). The first group is the *master teacher* group. These are the dedicated, inspiring individuals who stand out in our memory as real teachers. They make learning enjoyable, fun, exciting, and at times even profoundly moving. They are never too busy to be interested in a student, and they always display respect and high regard for them. They are genuinely concerned about pupils and treat them as equals on a human level.

They know their subject area extremely well, are enthusiastic about it, and are able to share and generate the same enthusiasm in their pupils. They encourage creativity, are able to tolerate differences of opinion between and among pupils and themselves, and can transform seemingly dull facts into vivid lessons. They manage their classrooms effectively, and expect their students to work and challenge them in the process. They try to be fair and impartial and generally have nonpunitive ways of dealing with discipline problems. In most schools, master teachers are few and far between.

Master teachers who burn out do so because they have dedicated themselves to their students and to the process of learning, perhaps to the exclusion of their own health. They work too hard, receive too little in the way of recognition or reward, and often eventually become disillusioned. When they finally stop to look around, they realize all their extra work and enthusiasm does not generate extra rewards and perhaps not even enthusiastic students. Some master teachers become administrators. This is unfortunate because it takes them out of the classroom, where they do tremendous good. However, there is no other form of advancement for a master teacher.

The second group of teachers found in any average school are the *rust-outs*. This group of teachers forms the core of the teaching personnel in many schools. They often enter teaching in the first place because it is easy to get in and they remain because no effective mechanisms for exiting are available. These teachers get the job done—usually. They may even be conscientious. But they are hardly an inspiration to their pupils, except at the end of the day when they resurrect themselves from the dead and get out of the school as quickly as possible. When a pupil asks this teacher why he has to learn math, the reply may be "Because it's good for you." Like brushing your teeth. It's drudgery but it has to be done.

Punishment is usually the accepted mode of discipline for the rust-out. So long as the vice-principal metes it out. These teachers are usually positively ecstatic over expulsions. Some of them encourage favorites and foster a great deal of competition because "that's what it's like in the real world." They believe education is for everyone so long as it's strictly academic.

These teachers made it through the system with little or no difficulty themselves, and wound up as schoolteachers, but they have little tolerance and no effective means of dealing with students who do not comply.

These kinds of teachers do not burn out from teaching. They are already rusted out. There is insufficient flow in the pipes and the remaining liquid has oxidized. Is it any wonder that many students hate school?

The third group of teachers constitutes, mercifully, another minority group. These are the *chronically miserable*. They see life and students through purple glasses. They continually scream, yell, and discipline students. Their stress levels are so high that they can neither handle students nor trivial incidents without overreacting. These teachers make learning a living hell for students. Their fuse is always lit, their buttons always pushed. Or, at another behavioral extreme, they may be withdrawn and abjectly depressed. These teachers are a menace to students and the learning process.

Sources of Mediocrity

Although the above descriptions are exaggerated somewhat to make a point, they are sadly often true. Why does this state of affairs exist in education? Some of the reasons are, I feel, as follows:

- The history of education in North America. The public has always maintained rigid control over teachers. In the process, as we've seen, teachers have evolved from lower forms of animal life to become comfortable, middle class citizens. If you keep your nose clean, you have a secure income, good holidays and a nice pension waiting for you upon retirement. Society actually encourages this mediocrity. Teachers dare not raise their voices nor discuss anything controversial in class for fear of reprisal. A newspaper article I saw recently indicated they wouldn't get the chance even if they wanted to:[1]

    > A publishing company says it will delete a paragraph about a child's suicide from a grade 11 school book because of complaints from board of education officials.
    > The paragraph, contained in a book titled *People in Perspective* and describing how a 10-year-old boy used the money he had saved for a bicycle to buy a gun and shoot himself, will be withdrawn in the third printing expected next year, said a senior editor at Prentice-Hall of Canada Ltd.
    > [The editor] said he discussed the matter with the author, who agreed that the paragraph was not essential.
    > The education director for the school board said he had received no complaints about the suicide reference but he and others decided the paragraph was unnecessary for discussion in the classroom.

    After several hundred years of struggle to get this far in the social order, why rock the boat?
- Teacher screening is either nonexistent or lacks vigor. Many businesses give elaborate psychological tests to recruit personnel for even minor positions. By and large, a systematic screening process does not exist for selecting potential master teachers. Some students enter faculties of education because there is nothing better for them at the moment or because they heard the courses are "Mickey Mouse."
- Teacher training is inadequate. I know of no other profession or trade where, after four or five years of training, one still doesn't know whether or not it is to be one's career. An electrician, for example, gets a good taste of the trade within the first few weeks of becoming an apprentice. But after five years of training as a teacher, I was totally unprepared for the day I walked into my first classroom. My experience is typical, not exceptional.
- Permanent certification is too easy to obtain. After one or two years of teaching at most, a decision must be made regarding the

permanent certification of a teacher. This is hardly sufficient time to judge the capabilities of a person in taking on the demanding role of a teacher.
- No real mechanism exists to deal with the rust-outs and the chronically miserable. These teachers draw the same rate of pay as a master teacher. This is so because the profession has unionized itself and teachers are paid according to years of training and years of experience, both of which are largely unrelated to effectiveness.
- Various teacher organizations are unions, dealing largely with contracts and the equalization of pay and working conditions. Although these functions are important, they do not publicly enhance the professional status of teachers.
- Certification of teachers does not lie in the hands of teacher organizations. However, this cannot happen until these same organizations provide an effective process of monitoring, maintaining, and enhancing effective teaching.

The rate of teacher burnout, rust-out, and drop-out will probably not shift dramatically in the upcoming years, except in a negative direction, unless dramatic steps are taken in a new direction. Only then will these problems be optimally low. They will never be totally eliminated, of course. Until then (and it may be a long while indeed before the necessary changes occur) we must be content to treat the problem of stress and burnout as we encounter it. But it's time that education started practicing preventive medicine.

The major thrust of any changes should be to develop teaching into a career, a life-long profession managed and maintained by a corps of master teachers who have more time to plan lessons and teach small groups of students. Means must be found to find and cultivate the talents of those who may be master teachers. As it stands now, this cannot happen. There must be dramatic changes made within the profession itself toward eliminating the conditions leading to teacher burnout, and improving the quality of education.

Too Many Cooks Spoil the Broth

There are far too many teachers. Other things being equal, the status of a profession is related to numbers. The more brain surgeons there are, the less status they have. The medical profession maintains rigid control over entrance to the profession. As a consequence, they attract intelligent achievers who strive for the goals the profession, by virtue of its control, can ultimately provide—standards of excellence, status, and high pay. Whether the latter two goals are desirable or not is irrelevant. They are powerful motivators in our society. If an occupation is to have professional status then prestige and money must accompany it.

This could happen for teachers, but it won't unless incentives are structured into the profession and potential teachers rigidly screened for their suitability to teaching. This is not a simple chore. There are a great number of studies which say very little of a consistent nature about the personality correlates of effective teachers. But that is due to a large extent to the "shotgun approach" of educational research over the last fifty years. Each time a new personality test was devised, someone tried to relate it to teacher effectiveness. The result was a confusing, sometimes contradictory hodgepodge of personality traits, each of which someone said was correlated with being a good teacher. More to the point, "personality" is too broad a term, and may not be the appropriate framework to assess teachers. There are diverse personality characteristics displayed within any subgroup, particularly one such as the master teachers.

A consistent theoretical framework is needed from which sensible hypotheses related to teacher effectiveness can be generated and then tested. With today's sophistication in testing, it should be possible to develop a matrix of powerful screening instruments that could be extremely helpful in predicting potential master teachers.

There are core conditions essential to master teaching. Teachers are currently trained as if acquiring knowledge of subject matter were all that counted. Teachers must satisfy requirements indicating they have completed a minimum number of courses in a major, but they do not have to satisfy any requirements indicating that they love children or that they even know how to talk to one, much less that they understand how to initiate the learning process in a child and take into account individual differences. They do not have to satisfy any requirements indicating that they themselves have a healthy self-concept, or that they can communicate effectively to a colleague or a parent. They do not have to meet criterion skills in disciplining students: "Just complete these courses, and you'll get your degree."

Teacher Training

"Anyone can teach" is a common expression. There is no control over the quality of the elements essential to good teaching when anyone, simply by virtue of completing specified courses, is allowed to begin teaching. And because teachers have been trained in numbers to meet the demands of population growth, then as it rises and falls, so does the fortune of the teacher. By allowing almost anyone into a college or faculty of education, tacit approval is given to a condition teachers vehemently attempt to deny later on.

But how can the problem of dealing with sheer numbers of children be met? By closely relating teacher training and real schools. Right now, teacher training occurs in a vacuum. For four years, a potential teacher drags him- or herself through endless hours of classes, writes papers to which are attached marks, and then, for several weeks around the second or third year of training, undergoes a torturous, artificial period known as "student teaching." Those few weeks are the closest that person comes to an actual classroom situation but, as all teachers know, it is not even close to being a realistic representation of teaching required in a classroom.

Suppose instead that in the first year of teacher-training, a student is assigned to a real school assuming real responsibilities. One of the first duties might be simply to take over playground supervision. This would give the potential candidate a taste of student difficulties such as fighting and swearing on the playground. (It would also free the elementary teachers for a well-deserved coffee break.) Now our potential teacher has a real problem on his hands. In fact, this sort of encounter would probably frighten many of the educational professors who for years have not dealt with actual children.

Assuming that difficulty could be handled, the student could then be given a choice—to be exposed, in the course of a year, to several theories regarding children's behaviors and be placed in a position to realistically attempt various approaches. At last, the relationship between a theoretical position and a genuine incident might be seen. Skinner, Ellis, Rogers, and even Freud would, in the potential teacher's eyes, begin to become "relevant." By rotating the teaching students through playgrounds, lunch halls, hallways, bus loading zones, and other supervisory areas usually handled by full-fledged teachers, exposure to both theory and practice could take place.

Ideally, the candidate should have to satisfy the school that he or she could handle such incidents fairly and effectively. Master teachers could model effective management procedures and ensure that students acquired their rudiments.

As students moved through their college training, they would be expected to handle more and more responsibility. In the second year for example, they might have to help with the development and scoring of teacher-made tests. They could then be introduced to the principles of evaluation and once again, the problem of transferring university theory into real life practice would be minimized. By the end of the second year, the student would once more have had real experience with an important part of teaching.

Throughout these years, effective communication with others— the heart of teaching—would be modeled and taught by master teachers and supplemented by course work and more practice at the university level. For example, if a student teacher were having real difficulty with a particular skill, he could be taken through an intensive session back in college so as to bring the skill to an acceptable level.

The rest of the training for young teachers could, and should, also be a balance between educational theory and functional application. Teacher training could be very realistic indeed. By the end of four years, a candidate could have sufficient exposure to teaching, to handling children and to the rigors of a school day so that the status of paraprofessional could be achieved.

Certification

Certification of teachers is currently in the hands of the government. Assuming a teacher obtains a job after training, then he must prove that he can handle a classroom for a year, perhaps two. If he behaves himself (and that's all that's really needed—not good teaching), a permanent "ticket to ride" is issued. Why such an appalling procedure exists is one of life's mysteries.

Even those individuals who have experienced a more realistic course of training as outlined above, would not be ready to assume responsibility for the future of a child. Their status should still be one of paraprofessional or intern. These paraprofessionals would assist master teachers for a period of two or three years on a day-to-day basis. They would teach classes about half-time, assist in making materials, diagnose and remediate learning problems with some students, and contribute to the overall planning of the learning programs of individual students. They would be paid, but only as interns.

Respect and concern for the child would be paramount. Where a child had difficulties, mechanisms for positive action would exist and be implemented. After such an internship, the paraprofessional could gain the status of *teacher*. He or she would then be entitled for certification.

But such certification should be controlled by educators, not bureaucrats. When I go to a doctor suffering from a pain in my leg, I have extremely high expectations—I expect to see a person who has had many years of training; I expect to see a person who has kept abreast of modern advances; I expect to see someone who can rule out various reasons why I might have this pain and arrive at an accurate diagnosis. Without that accuracy, I might die. After the diagnosis, I expect to have the most reasonable advice possible that will serve my best interests. Throughout, I expect the doctor to treat me like a human being and explain what he is doing. I also expect to pay dearly for all this.

But when my child enters school, my expectations are not as dramatic. This is so because all parents have experienced the educational system themselves. In addition, they read about schools and they see for themselves the sort of person a teacher is in our society.

As a result, parents expect that a teacher will do only two things: teach basic subjects and teach the child how to get along well with others. These are fairly minimal expectations. Even so, teachers are often poorly prepared to do either. It is *not,* however, the fault of teachers. They often do a heroic job given existing conditions. The fault lies in the fact that educators have not clearly been given the mandate to take the child's life in their hands, and through their skills, mold and shape the child into a fully individual human being capable of actualizing his or her potential. This is so because education is not an agent of social or personal reform. It is a ship that merely follows the winds of change. About every twenty years the winds shift, first from a humanistic base with cries for individual expression, and then to a more basic approach with cries for more discipline and academic rigor.

Every teacher is caught in the middle of this. State educational agencies and regional committees respond to the academic pendulum by changing the goals and objectives of curricula and by changing the content of courses. This is generally done fairly quickly with little time or money given to preparing teachers for the changes in emphasis, or for mechanisms which would ensure that the intended objectives would in fact be met. Also, little attention is given to improving and "fine-tuning" effective practices which may already exist.

To change this, teachers must take command of their future. They must know themselves where they are heading and how to take their students there. In order to do so however, a system must exist whereby the good teachers who already do this are not overshadowed by the mediocre and the inept.

The Master Teacher

As it stands now, a novice teacher entering into his or her first teaching position is left to fend for him- or herself. There is no means offered to draw the new teacher into an understanding of the educational process. A beginning teacher on a staff listens to and models those around him. Who else is there? Sadly, the models may often turn out to be rust-outs, many of whom are extremely negative and sour. As one teacher recently told me, "I'm leaving at the end of this year. I look around and I see these guys and I don't want to end up like them after ten years." This remark comes from a person who had been teaching three years. Each year, he showed more potential as a teacher. But what an environment he worked in. There was no hope, no positive ideal, nothing more to aspire to. The staff were by and large hopelessly negative and reinforced each other's views day in and day out.

Once the status of *teacher* is gained, the individual should still have a goal to shoot for—that of master teacher. The concept of master teacher offers a positive means of changing the less desirable aspects of the profession.

It takes a great deal of time for a teacher to know a pupil, to begin to understand his or her strengths and weaknesses, and then to accommodate and plan for those inevitable individual differences. By the time this happens, if it does, the student either passes on to the next grade or the teacher labors under exhaustion. It takes a great deal of time to plan lessons that truly accommodate individual needs. Most teachers receive no such time. As a consequence, they look for packaged materials that are easily prepared. Many teacher aides (when a school has them) are stuck running off ditto sheets. It's painful to watch a child come home with this drivel.

In order to minimize this very serious problem, master teachers would require a pupil teacher ratio of about fifteen to one and a reduction in teaching time to allow for program planning, curriculum development, research, and writing. An acceptable ratio of teaching to planning would be about half and half. And as for the pupil teacher ratio, recent research indicates that when current class sizes are reduced by half, student achievement rises.[2] The advantage rises sharply for a class of fifteen students and below. The factors that partially account for this, according to the researchers, are that students are better able to listen and respond, feel more relaxed, enter into more discussions, exhibit fewer behavior problems and can act more as participants than observers.

For financial reasons, no school board would ever support a fifteen to one student/teacher ratio and 50 percent less teaching time *given existing conditions*. But if the suggestions given here were implemented in an integrated fashion, then the scheme would not have to become a financial burden. By having fewer teachers and more personnel such as interns, aides, and in-training volunteers, the ratio could be reduced to acceptable levels and master teachers could have the time they need to plan and write. Master teachers should be paid accordingly. They would produce and write their own materials. There could be closer tie-ins with universities with master teachers contributing to teacher training and to the development of research studies serving the needs of their school.

Curricula would also have to change. Presently, education is basically knowledge acquisition with little time actually devoted to learning higher level skills such as planning, critical thinking, evaluation, and synthesis. School systems are by and large geared to academics. Students whose backgrounds are not average middle class or who are nonconformists in other ways are penalized. From the beginning, schools would have to recognize that there are multiple areas of human talent that should be encouraged to unfold. Acquisition of basic subjects, important as they are, must be taught in conjunction with a system encouraging the development of skills such as creativity, decision making, communication, projecting future developments based on current knowledge and so on. Calvin Taylor and his associates at the University of Utah have been working on the development of such a curriculum for many years.[3] The time is ripe for wide-scale use of many of his ideas.

"Master schools" would be the products of master teachers. They could provide students with well-developed skills, a vivid sense of the past, and preparation for the future. And they could do so on an individual level, taking into account the abilities of the student and his or her needs and talents, background, aspirations and so on. Currently, schools are forced to "teach to the middle."

Master schools currently do exist. But they are the exception, not the rule. And the master teachers on staff burn out because the other essential components required to carry out that function are missing. The class sizes are too large and teaching loads are excessively burdensome. All planning and development must be done on the teacher's own time. And there is no salary recognition or status in addition to what any other teacher might make.

School boards, the servants of the public, still maintain powerful controls over education. Such controls will never be passed to teachers themselves as long as the profession remains the unionized body it is now with no thrust toward true professionalism. The concept of a master teacher system, with all the other components intact, would enhance and maximize all the positive aspects of contemporary education. The net result would be a sharp increase in the quality of education.

The burnout and teacher dropout problem would be minimized (although other personal methods of coping with stress to be discussed later would have to be maintained). I can hardly imagine students hating schools in such a system. Another consequence therefore, should be a sharp drop in vandalism and attacks of violence and aggression toward teachers. Teacher absenteeism would also drop to an acceptable level.

The graduates of master schools would have had, for a period of twelve years or more, models of personal living, coping and thinking vastly different than today. They should be happier students with well-developed methods of handling pressures and demands. Perhaps many more creative ways of enhancing the quality of life for all would be the net result.

Chapter four

You Say Johnny Can't Read?

There are both internal and external reasons for teacher burnout. In the previous two chapters, I explored what I consider to be deep rooted problems inherent in the profession itself. These must change from within if ever the problems of education, including burnout, are to dramatically improve. There are external problems also over which teachers have no control whatever and may never control.

One problem already discussed is the control the public exercises over schools. Control must pass to teachers themselves, provided they have the kind of system and personnel who can handle the responsibility. In the future it would be good to see school boards, as they currently exist, die out. This does not mean the public should have no say in education. They should. But boards should consist of representatives of local master teachers, master administrators, the superintendent, and an elected public official. This group should make decisions on budget, policy, and other matters of educational concern. Because education is publicly funded, then a measure of government control will always be present.

Mutual Responsibility

The development of a child is shaped in very powerful ways by his environment in the first few formative years. Even though students enter grade one with different abilities, interests, and language competence, they are all expected to read at a grade one level by the end of first grade. Moreover, social expectations naively suppose that schools should somehow "equalize" every student, despite individual differences and all the disparity and change that accompanies modern living.

Recent research indicates that some students, particularly boys, may not be ready for reading until they are nine years old. Even so, they are all forced to read. Once a child has difficulty with reading, the initial reaction is one of panic. The parents feel it is the teacher's responsibility to keep their child at "grade level" in reading and other subjects. The parents may blame the school for the problem but they may also blame themselves. The teacher, in turn, may blame the parents, absolving himself in the process, or he too may feel guilty because a child in his class has difficulty in reading. Too often, each side blames the other and feelings of guilt are generated. Meanwhile, the reading problem continues.

The key to successful resolution of the problem lies in the appropriate attitudes of both sides. If the parents and the teacher can admit there is a problem that needs to be solved, and if there are competent resource specialists available who can diagnose and remediate as well as excellent remedial teachers available who can follow through on the recommendations, then there is an excellent chance that the problem will be overcome.

Teachers are not often trained to detect academic problems. Yet they are expected to be remedial experts and to be able, without training, to handle a variety of exceptionalities and handicaps. One teacher put it this way:[1]

> I've been teaching for eight years. Every year there seems to be a big change. Now they want to put exceptional students into the mainstream. I'm not against it. I think it's a good idea. But I don't have the training to handle it. And I can't see this particular system providing me with the necessary in-service either.

Another teacher, a special education teacher for five years, was more blunt:[2]

> I've had it. I left teaching to sell real estate because I'm totally wiped out. Special education: they throw you a roomful of handicapped kids and tell you to go to it. I had no formal training at all. A consultant appeared every two months and the staff resented me because I had fewer students than they did. Some of the parents expected miracles and some of the kids were such behavior problems it was unreal. They just dumped them all in one room—that's all it was, a dumping ground. I'm much happier now. I make a lot more money for the effort I put in.

Still another wrote:[3]

> I'm totally frustrated. I've worked with Michael for four years now and he's just slow. The parents won't accept it. They blame me and the school. They let him know too, because he comes in here and talks about it. He tells me openly that I'm incompetent. What am I supposed to do? Now I hear that the parents are going to sue us for not providing him with an education. What a joke! Can we sue them for not providing emotional support?

There are two sides to the coin of course. Sometimes, even if a teacher knows a student is having difficulty in a particular area, he won't bring it to the parent's attention, or will downplay its seriousness for fear it may reflect on his own competence. Is it then any wonder that embittered parents, especially those with handicapped students, write comments like this:[4]

> I find it difficult to trust any professional doctors—social workers, school administrators, psychologists, therapists, or teachers. It is my opinion that their main function, besides being paid, is categorizing and keeping handicapped children in their appropriate boxes. My child's teachers and school are doing more harm than good. At first, I played their [professional's] game, complimenting and thanking them for any semblance of education they morseled out to my child. When I saw my child falling further behind, I began to gently make suggestions that I knew from experience would stimulate my child's thinking. I was shut out by the professional staff who "naturally knew best."
>
> Now I write notes, make demands, consult lawyers, and do anything else in my power to put some fire in the dead situation in which my dear child is drowning.

Parents usually either overreact to a reading problem with too much anxiety and pressure to "cure" the problem quickly or underreact by showing no concern at all, perhaps believing that the child will outgrow it. Another view often expressed is, "It runs in the family. His Dad was just like that too."

The answers to why so many students can't read is not forthcoming. The problem is an extremely complex one. No solution is possible when one side blames the other or finds excuses for why nothing needs to be done. This is not the time for war; it's the time for teamwork to solve a mutual problem.

There are many instances where success in reading occurs because of excellent remedial help. There are many other instances in which the reasons for reading problems have gone undetected for years and the child has come to mistakenly accept the notion that he is merely lazy.

But what has all this to do with teacher stress? Good academic achievement occurs as a result of the combination of home and school factors. The stress of being scapegoats for "declining standards" is something teachers should no longer have to bear.

The Effects of Divorce

The skyrocketing divorce rate is a social dis-ease over which teachers have no control. (In California, it is approaching 50 percent of the marriage rate.) The result has been that classrooms are loaded with young single-parent children struggling to cope with the effect of this major upheaval in their lives. Although many "intact" homes have major problems too, divorce usually affects a child profoundly, but the extent of its impact depends on the age and sex of the child, the degree of family disharmony preceding the divorce, the personalities of the parents, the kind of relationship they have with the child, the capabilities of the child in handling stress, and the kind of emotional support provided by other family members.

While, as one researcher put it, "it is difficult to separate the effects of divorce from those of the prolonged trauma and strain preceding it," it is possible to quantify some of the effects.[5] The records of sixteen children (ten boys and six girls) were examined, the parents of whom were divorced during their nursery school years. Their behavior was compared to children not experiencing the trauma of divorce. Ten children (62 percent) exhibited acute behavioral changes which presented management problems for the teacher. Three of the children (19 percent) did not display acute symptoms but displayed other damaging emotional reactions. There were no changes observed in only three of the sixteen children.

These results contrast sharply with other researchers who report an incidence rate of only about 20 percent. The difference may be due to the fact that in the other studies, the mothers were asked whether their children's behavior changed as a result of the divorce, whereas in this study they were observed directly by the teachers.

Perhaps the three children who were apparently not affected handled the problem in such a way that the intense feelings of guilt, anger, and blame were worked out in healthy, adaptive ways at home. More typically however, the children reacted in negative ways, with sadness and anger, shock and depression, denial and regression. They occasionally became noisy and restless. They could become aggressive as well and revert to pushing, kicking, hitting and sometimes, biting. The regression and disorganization were more severe for two of the children. One of them wandered about aimlessly, crying, apparently bored and detached. He would lose his personal belongings and become unwilling to dress or undress himself. He made insatiable demands for approval. The other child, a girl, grew irritable, tearful, tense, bossy, and lost all interest in play. She would wet and mess her pants, suck her thumb, and chew her hair and the stuffed animals she brought to school. There were further indications of psychological and emotional disturbance:[6]

> [She asked the teacher] to readjust her clothing and to retie her shoes many times a day so that they would be tighter and tighter, apparently to heighten sensation and awareness of her body. She would pull up her underpants as high as she could, severely irritating the skin of her perineal region. She appeared to be masturbating in this way and eventually began masturbating openly with a dreamy, faraway look in her eyes.

This girl was referred for psychiatric treatment and responded well in about three months. The boy was also referred but did not make as much progress.

Finally, another group of three girls displayed quarrelsome attitudes, bossiness, and pseudo-mature mannerisms as a way of dealing with the stress. Concludes the researcher, "For some girls this may serve as a way to ensure the mother's love (i.e., by identifying with the 'wife of the husband who leaves home') during a period of intense emotional strain. . . . The persistence of this bond between them and their mothers signalled future adjustment difficulties."[7]

Though it is completely beyond the control of schools, divorce can seriously disrupt a child's progress in school. If teachers are to appreciate and handle the depth and complexity of these problems, they must be prepared either through training while in school or through in-service instruction.

factors Beyond the Control of Schools

Most people do not fully appreciate the tremendous emotional pressure on a teacher, particularly elementary teachers. Political realities such as the emigration of foreigners to North America have produced astounding numbers of students entering school who do not speak English. Add to this the numbers of Blacks and Spanish students (along with the general lack of appreciation of different cultures by many teachers and parents) and you have a mountain of dynamite on your hands.

The number of children who remain in school far exceeds the numbers of the late thirties. In 1936, only 26 percent remained in school throughout the twelve-year tenure. About 90 percent of the students who are presently entering the first grade will enter grade twelve eleven years hence.[8]

This means that teachers must deal with educational problems from an entirely different base than before. At the same time, there has not been a steady development of alternatives such as vocational and special education facilities to meet all the varying needs. Spending is tightly controlled and teachers are expected to do their best under the circumstances. This means that education, the one social institution that could really make a difference to the future, cannot even grapple with the present.

For almost every school system in North America, the problem of the junior high school potential dropout has to be faced. For a number of reasons, most of which relate to our expectations about academic gains, many students of junior high age have serious problems. For about 10 percent of them, the problems are so serious that they have become "pre-delinquent," if not actually delinquent, in their behavior. They hate school and most teachers with an intensity difficult to fathom for the middle class "average" teacher. Such students lack a sense of internal discipline (at least for school), vandalize property, use language that would peel the ears off a sailor, and are continually involved in conflicts. This kind of student nurtures a self-image as an "antihero." They become tough and rebellious, and their behavior is reinforced by a small group of peers similar to themselves.

Our present educational system simply does not prepare teachers for this kind of student. Fortunately, there are teachers in schools with the personal qualities and understanding necessary to deal with them. They often become special education or resource room teachers. But the burnout and dropout rate for these teachers is very high. At the junior high level in particular, the emotions can be very intense and demanding. Facilities are often inadequate, with makeshift classrooms operating out of broom closets, warehouses, church basements, old hospital rooms and the like. In many cases, despite the odds against it, the alternatives achieve a degree of success. There are still dropouts and suspensions, but for many students there is at least the glimmer of hope that they can succeed with something that is academically oriented. Too many boards and too many teachers would still rather deal with this kind of student by expelling him. These attitudes serve to keep education in the Dark Ages at a time when, as never before in our history, we require an orientation to the future.

The Decline in Student Achievment

Teachers are constantly being chastised for the supposed decline in student achievement. In the last few years, there have been outcries from various sectors, such as industry and universities that standards are dropping. This has been widely interpreted by the public and the media that student achievement is not what it used to be. College professors point to the abysmal lack of punctuation and sentence structure in student composition. From that, sweeping generalizations are made about students' capabilities. The implication is, of course, that teachers just aren't doing what they're supposed to be doing.

However, student achievement is not declining. Study after study supports that statement. For example, a recently commissioned investigation into the matter was conducted. A report was released stating that:[9]

- In the period 1956 to 1977 the performance of students in one large city, Edmonton, in the basic skills (reading, writing and arithmetic) was either the same in 1977 (arithmetic) or slightly better (reading) than in 1956. The same test was used on both occasions but separated by 21 years. If anything, students should have done worse on what were surely outdated items.
- Performance in reading in all grade levels tested (3, 6, 9, and 12) was satisfactory.
- Performance in number facts and operations were satisfactory at all grades tested. Performance in problem solving, geometry, measurement and consumer math was unsatisfactory. The latter however, are not well stressed in the curriculum.
- Performance in science was satisfactory at all grade levels tested.
- Performance in high school social studies (grade 12) was unsatisfactory in certain areas. MACOSA (Minister's Advisory Committee on Student Achievement) observed that there is however, no clearly specified core curriculum in social studies.
- Performance in writing and the mechanics of writing were generally unsatisfactory when tested by multiple choice items, but performance in these skills were considered stronger on longer assignments when students had to use their own words to write stories, descriptions, and arguments.

In recent years, there has been a shift in the Language Arts/English area toward the expression of ideas. There has been admittedly less emphasis on mechanics, such as punctuation and spelling. The results of the report seems to support that this shift in teaching emphasis has had an effect on what might be termed "page aesthetics." However, one can hardly condemn student achievement in general because of mechanical faults. The content of what one has to say surely counts for far more than technicalities. This is not to say that students shouldn't learn how to punctuate. Of course they should. And there should be more demands made on them in this area. However, as I sometimes point out to people, Sinclair Lewis won a Nobel Prize in literature despite the fact that he was a very poor speller. He had a good editor. Good editors are what's needed, not avenging angels of misdangled apostrophes.

The committee concluded, after reviewing available research on the factors affecting student achievement, that, "... home environment, aptitude and other non-school factors are perhaps as significant as instructional factors in affecting student achievement."[10] All teachers and school psychologists know this; they deal with it daily.

The Damaging Home Environment

Three examples serve to illustrate this point (the names are fictitious):

• The first concerns a thirteen-year-old girl who entered the sixth grade while under the care of a foster mother. We will call her Cheryl. Her natural mother was an alcoholic and constantly displayed feelings of ambivalence towards Cheryl. She would first reject the child, beat her, and chase her out of the house. Then, in her sober moods, filled with guilt and remorse, she would express motherly love and the situation would be more or less normal for a period of time. This disruptive ambivalence existed long before Cheryl entered the first grade. She immediately had difficulty with basic subjects and went through the usual diagnostic and remedial services available in her school system. Despite remedial help, she did not progress at all.

By the time she entered grade six, she had already failed once and was functioning at no better than a mid grade two level. At this point, she was taken from her natural mother by government services and was under the care of a concerned, empathetic foster parent. Cheryl was placed in a class with an excellent teacher who took the time to care and to make every attempt to individualize her program.

Cheryl's self-concept was abysmally negative. She saw herself as a person who couldn't do anything and who, moreover, didn't deserve any kind of help. With the help of her sixth grade teacher, her foster mother, and a good diagnostic program, Cheryl made fantastic academic gains. In some areas, she came right up to a grade six level. She still required help and would have received it in the resource program in grade seven. The home situation had been brewing all the time, though. Cheryl's natural mother called her occasionally indicating that she wanted her back. This created great stress for the child, resurrecting her old feelings and the vicious circle around which her life already revolved.

That summer, Cheryl returned to her natural parents. There was nothing that could legally be done to alter the situation. Cheryl is now a teenage hooker, walking the streets of a large city. The school did all it could but powerful life forces prevented an optimistic resolution of her situation.

• The second example is of a boy, Michael, who experienced difficulties in school right from the beginning. His home situation, unlike Cheryl's, was emotionally far more stable but still not conducive to good academic progress. Michael's father saw no real need for school, since his own experiences with it had been disastrous. He quit school in the eighth grade and despite his lack of formal training, made a great success of himself as a mechanic. He eventually set up his own business. Michael was not particularly interested in mechanics, but more important, he was spoiled and never had to face the consequences of his actions.

An attempt was made to place him in a vocational school, but his attendance was so sporadic, the school threatened dismissal. Instead, Michael quit on his own. He found a job on an oil rig, but when his employer found out he was not yet eighteen, he was fired. Michael is currently both unemployed and out of school.

- The final example is one in which parental refusal to acknowledge that their child had learning problems served to inhibit both emotional and academic growth. Danny is of average intelligence. His parents are fairly well off financially. (His father works for an oil company, and the family takes frequent vacations.) Danny is the youngest in the family. It is probable that his difficulties began long before he entered school. When he did, he immediately experienced academic difficulties. The mother refused to let him have any remedial help. In the second grade, the problem became worse, but again his parents refused to allow the child to have special assistance. In the third grade, the mother reluctantly allowed a part-time resource room placement. Danny was given an extensive battery of tests and an excellent individualized program was undertaken by a superb remedial teacher, but he failed to make progress of a significant nature.

In grade four, Danny was given even more resource help but he continued to make little or no progress. He became more negative and belligerent daily. His resource teacher knew there were emotional problems but was at a loss as to what to do. In desperation, she referred the family to a private agency. The father, who was quite sensible, convinced his wife they should follow through. He discussed his fears privately with the psychologist, stating he hoped something could be done to prevent his son from becoming a delinquent. The mother was extremely reticent, and apparently angry. Neither of them revealed much of the family dynamics.

Danny himself was unable to express much about the family situation. The psychologist had him do some projective drawings, a very useful technique in such instances. They did indicate Danny's perception of tremendous family conflict and his own stunted emotional development. There were indications that he would benefit from psychotherapy, but his parents were reluctant to give permission to proceed along those lines.

These examples illustrate some of the economic, family, and psychological pressures contributing to poor student achievement and dropout rates. These factors are beyond the control of present school systems.

Many parents have abdicated parental responsibilities and expect teachers to handle everything. Middle class parents in particular are caught in the endless pursuit of material things, victims of *Type A* patterns we continue to reinforce in North America (See Chapter 6, p. 51). Both parents often work to support mortgage and car payments, to pay for stereos, televisions, furniture, and all the peripheral items we value so much. The net result is little time for quality interaction with children. Schools cannot make up for this.

Does this mean educators need not change? Of course not—our school systems could be doing a lot better if the public were more aware and demanding of alternatives and were willing to spend the money to create them.

As it now stands, parents expect their children to attend school to learn basic academic skills. This in itself is an extremely narrow viewpoint. Within that viewpoint then, when their child has persistent difficulties, there are few alternatives to try. The ones that are attempted are often patchy, sporadic, and poorly integrated. The parents may try one service after another and finally collapse under the pressure of unrealistic expectations and an incomplete understanding of alternative possibilities.

Neither the teacher nor the parent is necessarily at fault. The child is the victim of the circumstances of the times and a system that perpetuates an unhealthy emphasis on academic subjects—often to the exclusion of other facets of learning. Since all that is expected from a formal education is the acquisition of rudimentary skills in language arts and mathematics, and since many students have difficulty with even that, there is a perpetual confrontation between parents and schools. On the average, teachers do a good job teaching basic skills. Illiteracy is declining in North America at a steady rate. But the problem is not one of merely increasing literacy. It is one of letting each student develop their many areas of skills and talents in a way that both allows maximum development of the child and does not burn out the teacher. There was a point in the early seventies when it looked like education might head in that direction. We will never know if it might have worked because the public mood changed and we are now in the midst of a depressing conservatism and backlash against education. This in itself contributes to teacher burnout by putting more pressure on the dedicated teachers who attempt to meet individual needs under the burden of large classes, little or no preparation time, limited alternative resources, and a public that constantly demands more and more but at the same time is willing to spend less and less for it.

Chapter five

Teacher Stress: Basic Theory

Stress may be either good (eustress) or bad (distress). It may come in insufficient quantity (hypostress) leading to "rustout" or it may come in too great a quantity, leading to burnout. It cannot be completely eliminated because that would mean entropy or death. To act as a guide in discussing the many aspects of teacher stress, see Figure 1 on the following page.

Figure 1 serves to conceptualize that a teacher faces stress from two major sources. Possible sources from the teaching profession itself are many and partially itemized in the *Stress Profile for Teachers,* while those from life events are itemized in two other scales, all of which are reproduced in full in Appendix A. Both major sources act and interact upon the individual teacher.

Individual differences among teachers has a tremendous effect, of course, on the *perceived* stress from the various stressors. Personality variables such as the chronic level of anxiety and neuroticism of a teacher as well as determinants such as age, sex, family history, and learning history all enter into the degree to which any one stressor will affect a person.

We all learn or are predisposed from an early age to react to stress in either effective or ineffective ways. Much of this depends on the modeling provided by one's parents and "significant others" in one's life. If one learns effective coping mechanisms then, as a general rule, neither teaching nor life changes create too much of a demand on our inner resources. Everything is handled in an easy, comfortable manner. Unless life events become overwhelming, such an individual enjoys good health and success in living, and actualizes more and more of his or her potential. There is minimal illness and long life until the body's machinery eventually wears itself out, as it must. If the coping methods are ineffective, then stressors, if continued, produce the symptoms of stress (behavioral, emotional and physiological) discussed in the first chapter. Should they continue, the individual may succumb to mental or physical disease. With some individuals, the negative cycle is so bad, the *disease itself* becomes the major (and perhaps only) coping mechanism!

Figure 1

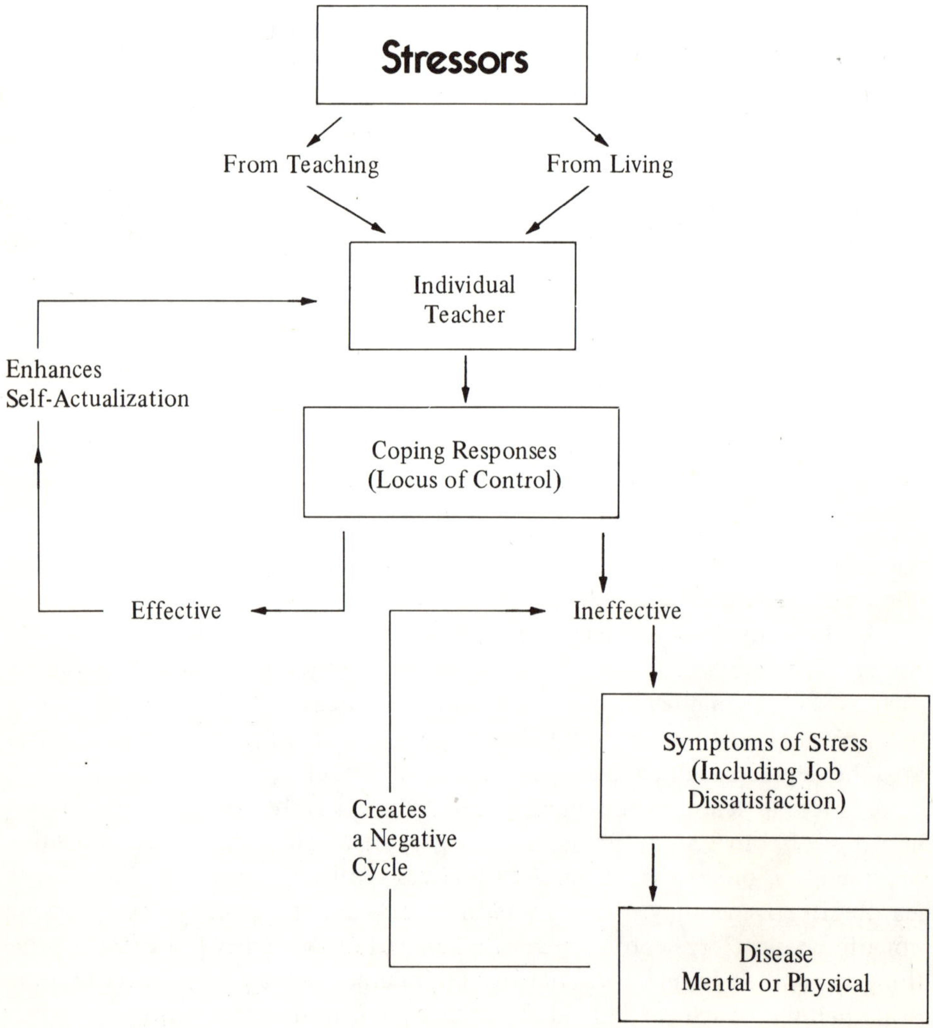

```
                        ┌───────────┐
                        │ Stressors │
                        └───────────┘
                        ↙           ↘
                 From Teaching   From Living
                        ↘           ↙
                     ┌────────────┐
            ┌───────→│ Individual │
            │        │  Teacher   │
            │        └────────────┘
  Enhances  │              ↓
  Self-Actualization ┌──────────────────┐
            │        │ Coping Responses │
            │        │ (Locus of Control)│
            │        └──────────────────┘
            │         ↙              ↓
         Effective              Ineffective
                                     ↓
                           ┌──────────────────────┐
                           │  Symptoms of Stress  │
              Creates      │   (Including Job     │
              a Negative   │   Dissatisfaction)   │
              Cycle        └──────────────────────┘
                                     ↓
                           ┌──────────────────────┐
                           │       Disease        │
                           │  Mental or Physical  │
                           └──────────────────────┘
```

Stress Is in the Eye of the Beholder

Adaptation to life's conditions is one of the most distinctive human characteristics. Yet we all do it so differently. Some ways are effective; others, though they temporarily relieve the problem, are not effective in the long run. Some psychiatrists tell us that life stressors provide "pivotal points" for developing good mental health. If the stressor is effectively handled, then the individual learns skillful coping behaviors and increases his general problem-solving capability. At the same time, if the coping methods employed bring only temporary relief, they too are learned. In the long run, however, these may well become destructive to the individual and reduce his emotional capacity and mental health. Consistent with this, Russell Hibler of Ohio State University found that high life stressors in elementary students are related to lower realistic problem-solving abilities.[1] On the other side of the coin, recent research from Harvard University indicates the importance of "mental wellness" to better health and longevity.[2] The study, conducted by Dr. George Vaillant, followed 200 men (students at Harvard in the early 1940s) for over four decades. Their adult adjustment was measured on such factors as job success, the happiness of their marriages and the number of vacations they took. Of the fifty-nine men judged as having the best mental health between the ages of twenty-one and forty-six, only two became ill (heart disease) or died (heart attack) by age fifty-three. But of the forty-eight who had the worst mental health, eighteen were either seriously ill or dead by the same age. This group suffered heart attacks, cancer, coronary heart disease, high blood pressure, emphysema, and back problems. One committed suicide. Dr. Vaillant concluded that good mental health keeps people physically well and helps them age more slowly.

What might generally be termed "attitude" is therefore crucial in dealing with stressors. An important component of this is the degree to which a person feels "in command" of his or her own life.

The Locus of Control

It is important to good health and good teaching that an individual feels "in control." The concept of the locus of control stems from J. B. Rotter's social learning theory.[3] It represents the degree to which a person feels that what happens to him—good or bad—depends on his own behavior (a feeling of internal control) as opposed to feeling it is dependent on chance, fate, or is under the control of powerful others (external control).

Very few studies have been carried out linking this variable to teacher effectiveness. However, numerous researchers have linked "internality" with healthy personality characteristics. "Internals" are generally less anxious, more trusting and less suspicious of others, more self confident and insightful and more willing to remedy personal problems. Not surprisingly, a significant relationship has also been found between internality and positive self-esteem. We would therefore expect internality to be closely associated with teacher effectiveness.

Internal locus of control is not something which is inborn. We all can learn to take more control of our lives.

What does this have to do with teacher stress? Almost all researchers who study stress in industrial settings cite evidence showing that feelings of alienation, job dissatisfaction, high absenteeism and other symptoms of stress stem from a feeling of external control. Most authorities therefore suggest that workers must participate in the decision-making process. This generalization most certainly applies to teaching as well.

Teacher Job Satisfaction

It seems obvious there is a close association between job dissatisfaction and teacher stress. However, this does not mean they are the same thing. A teacher may be quite dissatisfied with a particular teaching position, yet be a very effective teacher and not particularly upset by the stress of the position.

Studies of teacher job satisfaction and dissatisfaction have been carried out throughout North America and Europe. W. G. A. Rudd and S. Wiseman asked teachers in the United Kingdom to list their chief sources of dissatisfaction.[4] They were: (1) low salaries, (2) poor staff relations, (3) poor physical facilities, (4) burdensome teaching load, (5) inadequate teacher training, (6) large classes, (7) feelings of inadequacy as a teacher, (8) lack of preparation time, and (9) the low status of the profession in society.

Another major study provides further illuminating information.[5] Eight hundred teachers in 21 school systems selected from both rural and urban centers were polled. This study, too, indicates that teachers are most satisfied with areas they feel they can control (such as "freedom to select teaching methods") and least satisfied with areas where there is virtually no control (such as "attitude of society toward education").

The teachers reported wanting (in order of preference): (1) smaller classes, (2) more preparation time, (3) increased paraprofessional help, (4) decreased supervision duties, (5) higher salaries, (6) improved physical plant, and (7) increased involvement in decision making. It is also noteworthy but unfortunate in view of its importance, that increased involvement in decision making was not highly desired as an area of change. Although teachers feel they must have a great deal of freedom with respect to teaching methods and materials, they certainly do not feel that way about involvement in decision making at a local level.

These studies and others make it clear that the concept of an educational training and teaching system of master teachers would make great inroads in alleviating the problem of teacher burnout and increasing job satisfaction. Without an active change toward this direction, the demands teachers everywhere are making will serve only to further alienate the public from educators. You cannot demand more money, more aides, fewer students and the like without at the same time actively ensuring that the quality of education will rise as well. Teachers should have better working conditions and facilities. They are *learning* conditions as much as working conditions. It is our children who suffer by not being educated under such conditions. But as a parent I want to see that my child is taught by master teachers. No parent should have to shop around seeking a good school.

Self Actualization

Abraham Maslow stands out in bringing to public attention a theory of positive human growth leading to a sensible goal, that of self actualization. His theory is important in illuminating a *direction* of human personal growth. Unless individuals have such direction, those who decide to step into the driver's seat may suddenly discover that they have nowhere to go!

Maslow postulates that man has a hierarchy of basic needs.[6] At the bottom of the hierarchy are the deficiency needs, divided into physiological needs such as those for air, water, food, shelter, sleep, and sex. Next come basic needs for security and safety. According to Maslow, so long as these "lower order" needs are not satisfied, the individual's attention will be fully focused on satisfying them. However, when these needs are taken care of, higher needs, which Maslow calls growth or "metaneeds" come to the fore. Metaneeds are all of equal importance and include the need for truth, beauty, goodness, aliveness, individuality, perfection, justice, playfulness and the like.

Maslow devoted most of his life to studying the self-actualizing person. Actualizing means the development of existing or latent potential. However, "self" is not clearly defined by Maslow, although it is apparent that "self" in his terms is the psychological self—a dynamic, changing entity striving to become all it can be.

Maslow found self actualizers consist of less than 1 percent of the population. The characteristics of those who had "arrived" may be summarized as follows:

- Self-actualizing people are usually over sixty years of age.
- They represent the healthiest members of the human species both physically and particularly, psychologically (so remarkable individuals like Byron, Wagner, and Van Gogh would not qualify even though they were highly successful and talented).
- The perceptual qualities of self actualizers are superior. They are less emotional and more objective in their decision making and judgment.

- They are spontaneous and creative, are less inhibited and have less need to mask their feelings.
- They display psychological integration (a low degree of self-conflict). They enjoy solitude as well as the company of others. They have a healthy self-respect.
- They are always dedicated to some work, task, duty, or vocation which they consider important.

Maslow emphasized that these qualities were not invented by him, but were discovered to be those qualities which self actualizers possess. Extending his findings about self actualization in general to teachers specifically he said:[7]

> ... Our teacher subjects behaved in a very unneurotic way simply by interpreting the whole situation differently, e.g., as a pleasant collaboration rather than as a clash of wills, of authority, etc., the replacement of artificial dignity that is easily and inevitably threatened; the giving up of the attempt to be omniscient and omnipotent; the absence of student threatening authoritarianism; the refusal to regard the students as competing with each other or with the teacher; the refusal to assume the professor stereotype and the insistence on remaining as realistically human as, say, a plumber or carpenter; all of these created a classroom atmosphere in which suspicion, wariness, defensiveness, hostility and anxiety disappeared. So also do similar threat responses tend to disappear in marriages, in families and in other interpersonal situations when threat itself is reduced.

The Personal Orientation Inventory (POI), designed to measure aspects of self actualization, has been widely used in clinical studies, including studies done on schoolteachers. Through them, we have been able to gather valuable information on the relationship between self actualization and teacher effectiveness. In accordance with Maslow's theory, these studies show that teachers who see themselves as self actualizers also perceive themselves as more competent. They are perceived by their students as more concerned than teachers who are low self actualizers. Self actualization can be considered an important attribute for teachers to develop and therefore should be part of teacher training courses and in-services. "The self actualizing teacher, by enhancing the attractiveness and minimizing the dangers, may create growth situations for students. This goes beyond positive classroom climate as a means to student growth rather than merely as an end in itself."[8]

A variety of techniques and methods are available, many of which, if placed in proper context, help to achieve more of one's potential. Adding techniques to one's life may or may not be desirable, at present. But there may well be a need to alter some of your own perceptions. If so, I would encourage reading in your areas of interest. "Reality" is a function of one's "internal schemata." What reality is to anyone develops from experience over the years and *determines in part what we select to see in the environment.* We then receive feedback on what we have selected in accordance with what we have chosen to see. This feedback provides information which either affirms the schemata or alters it in some way. The rigid person however, is forever locked in a cycle of only selecting information which fits the preexisting structures he or she adheres to.

Many of us may never achieve total self actualization. Maslow found that only a very small percentage of the population actually "arrived." And there are criticisms that can be made of the theory itself. However, it seems to make sense that each of us have strengths and insights which can be developed more than is currently allowed in our time-bound world; that there is a world to enjoy and beauty to experience in the present moment; that material goods bring momentary pleasure but no lasting happiness; that we can all work toward a goal of achieving contentment and purpose; that there is an "art of living" which can be learned; and that this art goes beyond merely "coping" or "surviving." As such, it is the *process* of becoming that is important, not necessarily the attainment of the goal. *This* is what is missing in education today.

Chapter Six

The Concept of Stress

The problem of teacher burnout has to be placed into the broader perspective of life in the twentieth century, a century that has been variously described as the Age of Anxiety, the Age of Discontinuity, the Age of Uncertainty, the Age of the Global Village, and the Age of Future Shock. It can also be called the Age of Stress.

The Age of Stress

Vast and sweeping changes have occurred in this century. These changes have brought with them dramatic shifts in our lifestyles, attitudes, habits, thoughts, beliefs, organizational structures, health patterns, and methods of coping. Along with this, dramatic changes have been made in terms of what society expects from teachers. As social dis-ease increases, it manifests directly in the schools and in the children—and teachers are expected to "somehow" solve all the problems.

Because we were born into this Age of Stress, many of us may not be aware of the incredible changes that have been occurring in this century. Karl Albrecht traces five major changes that have contributed greatly to stress and burnout among all industrialized nations and their people.[1]

From Rural to Urban Living

In 1900, only 40 percent of Americans lived in urban areas. By 1975, this had almost doubled to 75 percent. Only 4 percent of the remaining 25 percent could be called farmers. And of course, the farmer of today works the land in a vastly different way than did his predecessors.

How does urban living contribute to stress? By *crowding* and by *pace.* Both these factors keep the urban dweller in a constant state of physiological arousal. Clearly the move from rural to urban living was also "a migration from tranquility to anxiety."[2]

From Stationary to Mobile

When I was a teenager, a group called The Fleetwoods sang a song about Jimmy Brown. It described the life of a small town boy who was born, married, and buried in the same small town. Even then, The Fleetwoods were being nostalgic, perhaps pining for an earlier, easier time. That way of life is no more. People move every three to five years. They change occupations as frequently. They travel extensively. Marriage and family life are subject to the same impermanence. People marry, divorce, and remarry. To say that all these dramatic life events are stressful is a dramatic understatement.

Time itself has become a packaged commodity in North America. Everyone wears a watch. There are clocks on all walls. Teachers and students rush from one class to the next, often with no time to even go to the bathroom in between. Stiff penalties accompany tardiness, not only in schools, but throughout our culture. We put a premium on efficiency and promptness, with no thought to the effects of rushing on our well-being.

A trip to almost any city in North America provides constant examples of frenzied productivity. The Interstates are dangerous no-man's lands, impossible to cross on foot, as the squashed bodies of animals give sad proof. At any time of the day or night there is the constant flow of truck after truck, car after car in a relentless, almost unbelievable passage of motion and energy.

The side road and hotel restaurants are remarkably efficient. Once seated, a waitress will be there to take the order—ready or not. A very few minutes later she will return with your breakfast. But there is a price to pay— the food is usually dull and tasteless, without restorative powers. It's just something to appease your stomach.

The situation is much the same in both America and Canada in many instances, but the pace is much faster in California and very obvious to an outsider. Going out for dinner in Calgary is a leisurely treat, a night out. Californians go out to eat more than not.

The night life is the same. Drink after drink is hurriedly served and quaffed, interspersed with disco dancing and nightclub "cruising" as partners are hurriedly sought for the night. "Good Timing" in America.

From Self-Sufficiency to Consumerism

Alvin Toffler describes the "throw-away mentality" that is now embedded in the North American life style.[3] This kind of life adds to stress by depriving us of any sense of permanence and stability. Perhaps that is why there is now such a nostalgia boom in North America. People are looking for a sense of security as well as antiques. Many restaurants spend lavishly in the attempt to recreate a sense of the past. Such a paradox.

From Isolation to Interconnectedness

"If you got it, a truck brought it." This slogan explains why truckers have a central place in our culture. The price of food now depends more on the price of gasoline than fertilizer. No longer do we grow our own food or assume any kind of self-sufficiency. We are connected in what can truly be called a global village.

Almost every North American owns a television. Worse, in too many homes it's always on. Toddlers crawling on all fours exploring their environment must soon come to grips with the rapidly changing world they see and hear from the box.

Researchers have demonstrated that watching television affects youngsters' outlook and their sensitivity. It affects their predisposal to violence and the quality of their family relationships. It affects children's imaginations, their self-image and the way they perceive others. (They spend more time watching television than they do in classrooms.) Television affects their reading, nutrition, and eating habits. Values, however distorted, are learned from television. Children learn that life and death occur in half-hour segments, duly interspersed with messages to buy food, cars, and beer.

Young people learn to live precariously on credit. None of this provides a model for long-term stress coping mechanisms, only short-term destructive ones. Faced with stress, many retreat to the momentary pleasures of alcohol and drugs. Or we eat. And eat. We drink coffee and cola by the truckload. Some suppress symptoms of anxiety with tranquilizers; when stress deprives us of sleep, we take pills, which in turn suppresses rapid eye movement activity (REM), the natural means for the body to release stress during sleep. Many people become self-destructive, uncaring, and robot-like in their dealings with others. They lash out in anger. Some cope by going to wild parties. The more tense the job, the wilder the party.

Television, radio, and newspapers further contribute to the feeling that we are living in a dangerous, hostile environment. The media distorts our perception of the world. It's interesting that heavy television viewers (as opposed to occasional viewers) believe the incidence of crime and violence is much higher than it actually is and that they see other people as being untrustworthy.[4]

From Physically Active to Sedentary

The majority of the work force now engages in work that is directly linked to information gathering and processing. That being the case, we spend most of the day sitting down. Then we climb into our cars, drive home and sit in front of the television.

Obesity is of frightening proportions. Few people have jobs that require physical labor. One hopeful sign, though, is the physical fitness boom in America. More and more office bound individuals are jogging or doing some other athletic activity regularly. Even so, the numbers of such people is still proportionately insignificant.

Our physiology was just not built for this kind of living. The accomplishments of modern medicine have lulled us into a false sense of security regarding our physical and mental health.

Stress and Disease

There is no doubt that stress-related diseases are the major killers in our society. In comparing the top ten causes of death in 1900 to the top ten in 1980, it is dramatically apparent that this is the case. Modern wonder drugs like penicillin, and universal inoculation have indeed almost eliminated bacterial and viral diseases as killers. But at the same time, heart disease, cancer, and cerebral vascular diseases have increased sharply. These diseases are all directly caused by or related to the effects of stress.

Life Change and Stress

Environmental challenges or stressors are measureable. We can quantify noise in decibels and we can measure psychological challenges in rating scales. This is exactly what two psychiatric researchers from the University of Washington Medical School did. Drs. Thomas Holmes and Richard Rahe interviewed 400 individuals. They asked them to rate various life events on a scale of 1 to 100 in which marriage was arbitrarily set at 50. The result of the ratings is in Appendix A, "The Life Stress Scale I."[5]

These researchers do not see any differentiation between positive and negative aspects of social change. "Change in financial state," for example, rates as 38 regardless of whether the change is a drastic gain or loss. From a common sense point of view, this flies in the face of personal experience. It seems much easier to handle a $20,000 inheritance than a $20,000 debt. Granted that a large increase in money can be stressful (some people winning large lotteries have dropped dead from heart attacks), on the average this should not be so.

The "Life Stress Scale I" has been around long enough and published in enough books to gather critics. Though not challenging the ranking method or the basic idea of the scale itself, researchers like Richard Hough, Dianne Fairbank, and Alma Garcia argue that positive and negative life stressors *do* produce different effects.[6] These researchers have developed a more detailed questionnaire than the Holmes and Rahe scale (see Life Stress Scale II). It includes more items and separates some of the original Holmes and Rahe items into their positive and negative aspects. Use of their scale will therefore produce a different set of rankings.

What is the relationship between life changes and illness? Holmes and Rahe indicate that the compilation of 150 life change units or less in a year will generate only a 33 percent chance of illness in the next two years. Higher scores bring greater risks. Scores between 150 and 300 yield a 50 percent likelihood while scores of over 300 increase the risk to 80 or 90 percent!

Subsequent studies using the Holmes and Rahe scale have been very illuminating. For example, in one study, it was shown that *ten times* more widows and widowers die in the first year after the death of their spouses than otherwise. Persons who are divorced have an illness rate *twelve times higher* in the first year after the divorce than do married people.[7] These figures illustrate the specific demands on the body from specific stressors. The point to be made is that change, whether good or bad causes stress, leaving people more susceptible to disease.

Life Change and Student Stress

There has been some research relating life changes to childhood woes. A definite link has been found between family stress and early academic problems. This has been extended to later social problems such as drug abuse, car accidents, and delinquency. A life stress scale for children has been devised using a procedure similar to the Holmes and Rahe method. This scale is reproduced in Appendix A as well.[8] It includes a distinction between desirable and undesirable events and some differentiation of each event on differing age groups. It could be a useful scale to administer to students in a confidential manner. The piling up of life stressors in children leads to manifestations we commonly observe in adolescents in particular—drug abuse, running away from home, and suicide.

Teachers and students are both victims of twentieth century living.

The Type "A" World: Stress and Behavior

It is not just change which produces stress. Our own behavior and thinking patterns have a profound effect on our health.

In 1974, a casual comment from an upholsterer who worked in their office inspired two doctors to trace the behavior patterns of their coronary patients. The observation that the upholsterer made was that the edges of the seats the patients sat in got the most wear, as if these people were living examples of the expression, "sitting on the edge of your seat."

The exhaustive research by Doctors Meyer Friedman and Ray Rosenman led to the publication of *Type A Behavior and Your Heart*.[9] The doctors came to the inescapable conclusion that the hurried "Type A" behavior pattern was linked to heart disease. The doctors characterized the

"Type A" person as an individual who is intense and aggressive. He has strong feelings of ambition and competitiveness. Most importantly, this person has a constant sense of time pressure—a race against the clock to always get things done. He is restless. Type A's are hard and productive workers, but they are caught in a never-ending cycle of too many things to do (many of which are self-imposed) and too little time to do them in. As a result, they constantly crowd more and more work into less and less space. "Polyphasic" thinking develops; this means trying to think about and do several things simultaneously (such as sitting on the can, shaving, and reading the morning paper all at the same time). The Type A person moves, eats, and walks rapidly. He often hurries the ends of sentences when speaking. He feels impatient with the rate at which most things take place. He even feels guilty about relaxing, which he considers to be "doing nothing." He thinks about business while on vacation. He tends not to listen attentively to others because he is constantly preoccupied with his own thoughts. He hasn't time left to enjoy the things that he acquired because he is too busy acquiring them or trying to keep what he has intact. More importantly, this person is afraid to stop doing everything faster and faster because he strongly believes that it was his feverish pace that led him to his accomplishments in the first place.

The Type B person represents a more positive personality style, one which is less stressful. Type B people don't have a frantic sense of urgency except when it is really needed. They value their leisure time, and work for personal satisfactions rather than just trying to beat out the competition. Consequently, they have no need to measure themselves and their self-worth against their peers or in terms of the numbers of achievements that they are able to make. They allow themselves time for quiet contemplation or meditation. They take the time to think through problems, to weigh alternatives, and to construct effective courses of action. In the long run they make fewer mistakes and are more creative than Type A's because they take the time to consider many approaches to a problem before making any decisions. They are not impulsive and are generally more thoughtful and original. They are equally competitive when they need to be, and in general have a less abrasive personality. All of us, of course, are a mixture of Type A and Type B; but generally, one of the two is dominant.

What is the fruit of the Type A personality's behavior? Type A individuals are more than *twice as prone* to the onset of clinical coronary disease. They are nearly *five times more prone* to a second heart attack and they have fatal heart attacks *twice as frequently* as "Type B" personalities. Traditionally, men have been more prone to heart attacks than women. Is this because of genetic and sexual differences or is it because of personality styles? Further research by the two doctors revealed that when women lead the same kind of stressful Type A lives as their male counterparts, their heart attack incidence increases to the same level as it does in men.

Type A behavior has accurately been described as "hurry sickness." This kind of personality pattern begins to show up in the early teens, especially in middle-class youth. The pressure to compete for top grades and college entrance takes its toll. Even now, teenagers occasionally have heart attacks and many young people certainly lay themselves open to greater risk at a later age.

Only 25 percent of coronary disease can be accounted for by the traditional risk factors of high blood pressure, smoking, cholesterol and heredity.[10] Therefore, an astounding 75 percent must be accounted for by other means. What are they? Can the link be made between change, behavior, and heart disease? Heart attacks, strokes, and other blood vessel diseases are the number one, three, and four causes of death. Cancer is number two.[11]

There is little doubt that much of this is due to our "Type A world," the whirlwind of twentieth century razzle-dazzle, and "hurry sickness."

The Physiology of Stress

No discussion of stress would be complete without some discussion of its physiology. No single researcher has done more to make the public aware of stress than Dr. Hans Selye. He is in fact, credited with coining the very term "stress." He is currently at McGill University in Montreal and has recently founded the International Institute of Stress to carry on work in this area.

According to Dr. Selye, stress is "the nonspecific response of the body to any demand made upon it."[12]

To understand this concept, think of a thermostat. A thermostat acts like a regulator. When it gets too cold in the house, the heat turns on automatically. Then, when the heat reaches a predetermined maximum, it turns off automatically. This is an example of homeostasis, keeping things in balance.

Keeping things in balance throughout the numerous, complex actions of the day eventually wears machinery out, whether it is metal or flesh and bone. There is a constant demand on a furnace and its regulator to keep the temperature at a certain level. Because we enjoy only its constancy, we tend to forget all the work needed to regulate it. So it is with our own bodies.

Stress is the *nonspecific* response of the body to *any* demand made upon it. What does nonspecific mean in this context? It means general demands for adaptation to unique environmental challenges. For example, when exposed to cold, we shiver to produce more body heat. When exposed to heat we sweat and the moisture has a cooling effect. The demands made to maintain homeostasis or constancy are stressful. Environmental challenges are stressors, which may be either physical or psychological.

It is immaterial whether the demand from the environment is hot or cold, pleasant or unpleasant, because the effect on the body is the same. A demand for readjustment, for adaptation, is made. Stress affects all living creatures. But the utter lack of stress means death.

All normal activity produces stress, because there is a demand for general adaptation. A game of chess, watching a play, running in a race, all produce stress. Selye points out that "The lash of a whip or a passionate kiss may be equally stressful in terms of making adaptive demands."[13] This is so because the body generally speaking has only *one and the same defense plan for all forms of stress.*[14] For every demand, every environmental challenge, the physical reaction of the body is the same. The endocrine glands and the autonomic nervous system (the involuntary nervous system) become the major defense weapons in the three phases of the *general adaptation syndrome.*

The General Adaptation Syndrome

The body goes through three stages in its fight against stressors. These stages are:

1. The Alarm Reaction. This stage consists of two phases. In the first phase, the body falters under the attack of the stressors. Messages are sent to the pituitary and the hypothalamus glands. From there, the body mobilizes its forces and enters the second, or defense phase of the alarm reaction.
2. The Stage of Resistance. Should the stressors persist, there is an adjustment that the body makes to them. We say we "get used to it." But there is a price to pay for the continued increased production of the stress hormones of the adrenal cortex (corticosteroids).
3. The Stage of Exhaustion. Should the stressors continue to persist without abatement, the body becomes unable to make adjustments and dies.

It doesn't matter whether the stressors are mental or physical, the stages of the adaptation syndrome are virtually the same. Unfortunately, we are not so finely tuned that we always react in a perfectly adaptable way to all stressors. The reaction of the body machinery can cease altogether. Sometimes the reaction may be too weak, other times it may be too strong; at times it can be incorrectly chosen. In any of these situations, the damage caused by the body's defensive systems may be greater than the original stressor. The body may be destroyed by its own protective mechanisms. It is for this reason that Selye has termed stress illnesses as the "diseases of adaptation."

Fight or Flight

Another important physiological response was delineated by Dr. Walter Cannon, a pioneering Harvard physiologist. When we are faced with stressors requiring immediate attention, the body produces an involuntary response which increases all of the following: (1) blood pressure, (2) heart rate, (3) the rate of breathing, (4) the flow of blood, and (5) metabolic rate. This response prepares us to meet the stressor—to fight or flee.

The response is easy to induce via psychological stressors. Experiments have shown that the elicitation of the "fight or flight" response leads to transient high blood pressure. Further research demonstrates that continued elicitation of the fight or flight response leads from transient to permanent hypertension.

However, it seems apparent that some people are much more adaptable to stressors than others. The degree to which we are internally adaptable makes a great deal of difference as to how we manage stress. Is it possible to increase the degree of internal adaptability? Some researchers believe this to be the case.[15] Just as the body involuntarily produces a "flight or fight" response, there may be a "stay or play" response which does the opposite. To do the opposite, such a response would have to simultaneously lower breath, heart, and metabolic rate as well as decrease blood pressure. There are techniques which anyone can learn that will do this. This is important because it means that we could learn to "fine tune" our nervous systems and become more adaptable in meeting the stressors of everyday life.

Faced with the continued escalation of stressful life events, all individuals must learn to adjust, adapt, cope, and overcome rather than denying, avoiding, or escaping stress. But positive coping methods, though extant, are not universally available. The effectiveness with which a person is able to handle the complexity of modern life is directly linked to his or her physical and mental health, longevity and enjoyment of life. So we turn now to methods for managing personal and professional stressors.

Chapter Seven

The R.E.A.D. Program for Managing Personal Stressors

The R.E.A.D. Program

In the previous chapters, we discussed some causes of teacher burnout in North America, and presented the principal components of both psychological and physiological stress. Because teachers function at the hub of our society, a large proportion of them have become the unintended casualties of the larger social dis-ease. It is obvious that the situation is not going to become less intense in the foreseeable future—in fact, there is every indication that the role of an educator will become an increasingly stressful one.

It seems apparent that if we are to survive this century, and if we are to go beyond that and cultivate an art for living which leads to enjoyment, contentment, and love for ourselves and others, then nothing less than an integrated approach will suffice. This is particularly true of those on the "front lines." The social and educational milieu, in all likelihood, is not going to provide the means for managing the stress of being a teacher. If one is to remain an educator, then the responsibility for maintaining one's mental and physical health is a personal one.

For this reason then, this chapter will present a personal system of stress management. In it, I will address you, the reader, directly. If the R.E.A.D. program is carried out fully, the probability that you will enhance your effectiveness in the classroom, with your colleagues, and at home will be dramatically increased.

The essential ingredients for this personal stress management approach are:

R — deep relaxation
E — regular exercise
A — attitude and awareness
D — diet

My attitude in regards to dealing with personal stressors is very much one of "cleaning up your own back yard." Ultimately, each of us must face the conditions of human existence alone, including death. No one can do it for you. Therefore, you must make your own choices about taking control of your own existence. It can be done. Reading about it can help set appropriate directions but if you fail to follow through, then not much will change. So, I recommend that you begin to R.E.A.D. Once you do so, you'll find that life can take on new perspectives and deep dimensions of enjoyment you may not have thought possible for yourself.

There are many methods available for each of these "ingredients." Find the ones that suit you best, but *put them all together*—gradually, at first. Don't kill yourself with good habits.

Deep Relaxation

As a consequence of our rapidly changing lifestyles and the addition of greater numbers of potential stressors, many North Americans have felt the need for safe and effective ways of unwinding. From the midsixties on, many forms of meditation and relaxation have become an integral part of the life style of hundreds of thousands of people. These techniques can be extremely useful provided they are kept in perspective. They are one of the four essential ingredients and are of two kinds, outside in and inside out.

Outside In and Inside Out

In Chapter 6, we discussed the physiology of the "fight or flight" response. In times of emergency, the body reacts involuntarily in such a way that the activity of the sympathetic nervous system (the "accelerator" part of the autonomic nervous system) is increased. Breath, heart and metabolic rate all increase and blood pressure rises as the body prepares to fight or flee. This automatic mechanism was necessary in ancient times as a means for coping with the dire conditions our ancestors had to face.

In the twentieth century however, we are usually unable to fight or run away from threatening situations either because of social constraints or the fact that often our adversaries are nebulous ones. Experiments have shown that although a person may display no outward signs of stress or anxiety, damaging physiological changes do occur inwardly. Without the normal "release valve" of fighting or fleeing, the body "turns against itself" as it were, producing various stress-related illnesses.

Any response which produces an effect contrary to the fight or flight response could therefore be a valuable ally in the body's defenses against stressors, provided it is wisely used.

Several techniques qualify in eliciting the "stay and play" or "relaxation response." This response automatically lowers the breath rate, the heart rate, the metabolic rate, and decreases blood pressure.[1] The presence of these physiological effects indicate the body is getting good rest.

When balanced with healthy activity, the cycle of rest and activity puts a person more "in tune" with the way nature appears to work—in cycles of rest and activity. We sleep and then work during the day. Bears hibernate in the winter and are active for the rest of the year. Buds lie dormant all winter and bloom in the spring. There are cycles within cycles. Each phase of rest is followed by a burst of action and then rest again. When rest is regular and routine, then activity is usually also more efficient. If the cycle is interrupted, then a disturbance in either rest or activity occurs. For example, if we have a poor night's sleep, our day's activities are not as efficient. If the activity is inefficient, getting rest again at night may also be disrupted. A negative cycle is created.

Relaxation techniques can be helpful in balancing these cycles of rest and activity. When a technique uses a physiological method for producing relaxation, I call it an *outside in* technique. This points out relaxation or inner repose is produced from an outer physical effort. When an individual uses some method of focusing inward, such as the use of a *mantra* which is employed in various forms of meditation, or psychological images used in various clinical techniques, then I call the method an *inside out* technique. A feeling of relaxation is produced and the body "follows" as it were, by becoming relaxed. Although the end is basically the same with either technique, the means are quite different. Some involve considerably more effort than others. Some take a considerable amount of time to perfect. Others involve dramatic changes in life style and habits. Others are the outer expression of various religious beliefs. Some are clinically developed, others have come from ancient sages in the Orient.

These techniques are not all the same. Even though similar physiological changes occur, it doesn't mean the techniques are identical. *And because there are differences, each technique has some place in the overall structure of things.* Each has some usefulness depending on the needs, circumstances, and preferences of the individual. What is important is that you need to choose what is best for you. For some individuals, some of the techniques available can become ends in themselves, with consequences contrary to their original function. *No one* technique is the answer to all problems.

Before discussing some of these techniques, a few guidelines and cautions are in order:

- Adding periods of relaxation to your life style may be an exercise in futility unless you straighten out any dramatic ups and downs you may be experiencing. Be aware of what is happening in your life and the strength of your coping mechanisms. You may want to use the questionnaires in Appendices A and B for this purpose.
- Never be afraid to ask for professional assistance. Experienced teachers in particular often have no one to turn to. Seek out the help you have confidence in. For some, this may mean a professional psychologist, for others a priest, pastor, or trusted friend.
- Practice on a regular basis whatever method suits you best. This seems to be very important. Variety may be the spice of life, but regularity is the main course. Just relaxing when you feel the need is not likely to produce the desired effects. Certainly once daily, particularly after work, is a good time to unwind.
- The periods of relaxation should be brief. Too much relaxation can be as harmful as too much activity. Certainly no more than a half-hour at a time should be spent at each session. When you are first learning, however, some methods may require more of your time initially.
- Remember that too much of anything is not good. We all thrive when our lives are balanced. Don't be caught in what Donald Dudley and Elton Welke call "the relaxation trap." You can become so preoccupied with "peace of mind" that you can neglect the diseases and disease symptoms associated with relaxation. These are illustrated on the following page in what Dudley and Welke have called the "Colter Coaster" (see Figure 2).[2]

The coaster effect is particularly important for teachers, since there is a lot of "coasting" between high activity during the school year and abrupt shifts to low activity over Christmas, Easter and summer holidays. If you are susceptible to any of the illnesses on the coaster, then you would do well to take steps to flatten out the cycles of rest and activity in your life.

Some outside in techniques are: (1) progressive relaxation, (2) diaphragmatic breathing, and (3) biofeedback. Some inside out techniques are: (1) various meditation techniques such as Transcendental Meditation (TM), (2) autogenic training, and (3) visualization. There is a great deal of literature on each of these techniques available at almost any bookstore. I have, therefore, picked a representative example of an outside in and an inside out technique for discussion.

Figure 2
The Colter Coaster

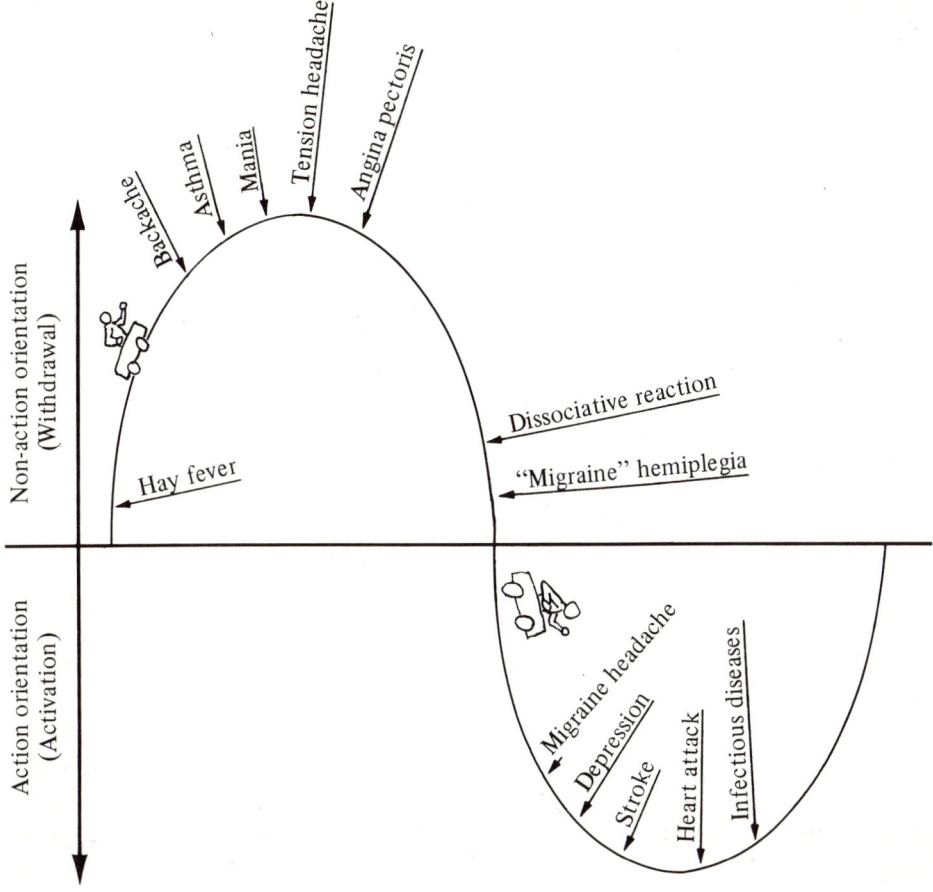

Some of the diseases which fit the coastering phenomenon. Most diseases vary in intensity with wide changes of activation and can begin during either the high or low periods. From *How To Survive Being Alive* by D. L. Dudley and E. Welke. Copyright 1977 by D. L. Dudley and E. Welke. Reproduced by permission of Doubleday & Co., Inc.

Progressive Relaxation

Edmund Jacobson might properly be called the "father of relaxation." Beginning with his work at Harvard University in 1906, relaxation techniques have been studied for potential use in reducing anxiety and in treating a variety of psychosomatic illnesses.[3] Jacobson spent most of his life trying to show that "to be relaxed is physiologically the opposite of being anxious."[4] He developed a method termed progressive relaxation (PR), a form of muscle activity reduction wherein the individual learns to ignore the *content* of his anxiety (its mental component) and relaxes instead the accompanying *neuromuscular* component.

In his work, Jacobson taught people to progressively relax different parts of their body. He also went beyond the medical value of progressive relaxation for specific treatment of anxiety and hypertension and viewed it as good preventive medicine. On this line of reasoning, he formulated various exercises designed to be incompatible with the stress of light activity. He called this "differential relaxation." His book is replete with occasionally humorous photographs of people with various parts of their bodies totally relaxed while other parts were normally "alert."

Jacobson was also able to teach a very few persons to reduce muscular activity to the point where, for all practical purposes, it was nil. He also found that mental activity disappeared during these moments. Although Jacobson did not call it such, this is what is meant by "transcending" in inside-out techniques like Transcendental Meditation. Jacobson noted the uniqueness of that particular experience and reported many positive health benefits. For instance, some of his patients *spontaneously* lost the desire to smoke cigarettes or drink alcohol to excess. These experiences correlate closely with those reported by many others using a variety of techniques. Perhaps "transcending" is the common basis for their effectiveness.

Following Jacobson, a number of other techniques involving relaxation have been developed for use in counselling and clinical settings. For instance, Wolpe's systematic desensitization (SD) is widely used, primarily for treatment of neuroses and specific anxieties.[5]

Virtually all the clinical techniques are variations in Jacobson's message that relaxation is the antithesis to anxiety. One can turn to a wide variety of books and find detailed instructions on becoming adept at one of these outside in methods. One variation of progressive relaxation is presented in Appendix C.

Transcendental Meditation (TM)

The TM technique became quite popular in the midsixties and early seventies. It is still around, but not receiving the public attention it once did. TM is a good example of an inside out technique. Basically it uses mental processes as a means of producing physical relaxation. While meditating in this way, the body relaxes automatically once the correct use of a specific thought, called a mantra, is learned. Instructors of this technique are carefully trained and courses are given in many countries. Because of the many semi-religious overtones of TM, Harvard researcher Herbert Benson isolated what he considers the essential components of TM and developed a clinical meditation technique.[6] He considers that any neutral thought can act as a mantra. His choice of "one" for this purpose has come to be referred to as the "Harvard mantra."

A unique state of consciousness is said to be experienced in meditation, one which combines rest with alertness. The process defies description, because it is a unique experience, but from a *psychological* perspective, like Jacobson's patients, many meditators find this experience a very positive one. It seems that incorporating a daily routine of "restful alertness" with activity forms the basis for a more stabilized, productive lifestyle, virtually free of the drastic ups and downs of the "Colter Coaster."

Many meditating schoolteachers have written to me of their positive experiences with TM. I did some research on the effect of TM on personality characteristics associated with effective teaching and found that TM did help to give teachers a healthier self-concept, less anxiety, and more of a sense of self-actualization.[7]

Despite my generally positive attitude toward Transcendental Meditation as a means to regulate rest and activity, let's put it into perspective:

- The claims of benefits from regular practice of TM are vastly overstated. Recent claims regarding "paranormal" phenomena, such as levitation, are simply absurd. Even though meditators and TM teachers talk as if these were perfectly normal things that happen every day to meditators, *there is no evidence whatsoever to support them.*
- Research studies used to support even the more modest claims, like reduced anxiety and greater self-actualization, though indeed exciting, are still preliminary in nature. The scientific method is a very cautious one. Many replications of an experiment are required before being accepted as "fact." Although hundreds of experiments have been done on various aspects of the TM technique, one could easily cite hundreds, even thousands, of research studies done on a given psychological test! The research done on TM so far is merely a drop in the bucket.
- The benefits of stress reduction can come from many directions, sources, and techniques. There is no exclusive source or ultimately "right" method.
- No one has isolated the components of what makes TM, or for that matter, *any* therapeutic technique "work."

Used wisely, a great number of relaxation techniques can bring relief from stress and a new sense of enjoyment.

As a final word, when I say "relaxation," I mean *deep* relaxation that counters the stress response. Taking a vacation, going fishing, watching television and so on are changes of pace and bring a sense of relaxation. They do *not* however, give the body what it needs to "unstress." For this purpose, one of the inside out or outside in techniques must be learned and incorporated on a daily basis in your lifestyle.

Exercise

The second essential component of any effective stress reduction program is regular exercise. To be effective, the exercise should be aerobic in nature (one in which you have to breathe heavily but which doesn't consume oxygen faster than your heart and lungs can supply it); it should be done regularly and it should involve ten to thirty minutes per session.

The essentials of any program of regular exercise are:[8]

- Intensity. This involves, as a first step, taking a "stress test" or an exercise test from a physician. You should, however, locate a doctor who is himself a reasonably good specimen of health and who is knowledgeable and supportive of exercise as a means of developing cardiovascular fitness.

  Taking the stress test will enable your doctor to set your level of exercise intensity. This is the level at which you will achieve an improvement in fitness but not encounter any danger to your health. Because we live such competitive lives, our first urge when exercising is to push ourselves to what may be dangerous levels. Slow down and take one step at a time. Intensity has to be set at about 40 percent of your personal capacity to result in a fitness improvement, and it is this capacity which must be measured on a stress test. Intensity should be set as low as possible in the early stages of a training program and after six months to a year, gradually increased to about 80 percent of capacity. More details can also be found in Kostrubala's book, *The Joy of Running.*[9]

- Frequency. Frequency is of less importance than intensity. It takes a minimum of two sessions a week to maintain fitness and three or more to see improvements.

- Duration. According to Drs. Howard, Cunningham, and Rechnitzer a program of twenty minutes per session (three times weekly) will result in weight loss. In the beginning stages, ten minutes is sufficient. This should gradually be increased to twenty or thirty minutes per session. They also say that fitness improvement is similar when exercises are performed at lower intensity and longer duration compared to high intensity and short duration. Once again, the advice is to take it easy and build fitness slowly and regularly.

- Type. The type of exercise is not too important as long as it is low-resistance and repetitive in nature. This includes walking, running, jogging, skipping, swimming, and cross country skiing, but low intensity activities like golf and bowling are not recommended.[10]

> Any activity will do quite well, as long as it is low in intensity (60 percent of maximum) and carried out for 20 minutes or more.
>
> In summary: It's necessary to train three times a week or more, at more than 40 percent of your maximal capacity, for at least 10 minutes per session, to realize a training effect. If weight loss is important, the exercise sessions should be as long as possible (30 minutes or more), with intensity kept as low as possible (close to the 40 percent).

The main effect of a regular exercise program seems to be protection against heart disease and hypertension. If a physically active person does have a heart attack, the chances of survival are three or four times better than their inactive counterparts. Kostrubala says in relation to jogging that "There has never been a proven death reported from coronary heart disease—a heart attack—in anyone who has finished a marathon within seven years after finishing."[11]

Physical exercise also reduces the incidence of other diseases and diminishes the severity of pre-existing diseases. In general, cardiovascular fitness increases until about eighteen years of age in men and fourteen in women. There is a gradual decline after that which physical training serves to slow down.[12] There are many instances where sixty-year-old active people are much more fit than their twenty-year-old inactive counterparts.

Finally, sustained regular exercise improves self-esteem, alertness, and zest for living—precious commodities (much more valuable than even the escalating price of an ounce of gold) in any time or place.

Attitude and Awareness

Attitude and awareness are both very broad terms but they are a third extremely essential ingredient in any holistic program of stress management. In the first place, we cannot change many of our behaviors without first changing our attitudes, and our attitudes won't change unless there is some general awareness that what we are currently doing needs improving.

In relation to a low stress life style, attitudes are important in terms of how we react to stressors, while awareness will tune us in to our own bodies and our environment. In this way, we can satisfy our own needs and those of others in the best interests for all concerned.

Probably the most important attitude we can develop in our hurried lives is one of taking it easy, taking it as it comes. This simple phrase is one taught to me several years ago when I first learned Transcendental Meditation. By applying it systematically to all activities, I found my lifestyle and general psychological state turning to much more of what is now called Type B behavior. I started to manage time more effectively. These sorts of changes have implications that go beyond teaching performance and into all aspects of living, tending to create a far more balanced lifestyle. By doing one thing at a time, the "polyphasic" thinking, characteristic of Type A's (and which I am convinced eventually destroys them) begins to dissipate. As a result, the ability to listen to others improves, as does concentration.

We can and should become more genuine in our feelings and actions and express this in a healthy way in our interpersonal relations. "Taking one thing at a time," "taking it easy," and "taking it as it comes" allows us to become more creative, more productive, more skilled at dealing with stressors, more appreciative of our environment, and a whole lot happier. In other words, mental calmness is an important ingredient in coping with stressors.

Stress Inoculation

If you can appreciate the importance of mental calmness to your well being, then you can understand the mechanics of stress inoculation.[13] The idea is drawn from the medical model in which a person is injected with a small dose of a harmful substance in order for the body to develop a tolerance and immunity to the larger stress—the disease itself. I. L. Janis, in applying this idea to psychological stress, says a person can develop "emotional inoculation" by going through the "work of worrying."[14] This is achieved by working through these three stages:

First, gather realistic information. You should become aware of the demands you will probably experience in a given situation. Being half informed however, can be extremely stressful as well. Get as much realistic information as you can, even if it's unpleasant information.

Second, when you begin to worry, get details of the resources available to you—resources that could help you cope more effectively with the situation. If there are no outside resources, then you should know that too. You may be able to do something about it beforehand.

The final step is to encourage yourself to make plans and to reassure or reward yourself for doing so. Accept the stressors in the meantime.

Suppose for example, you are a beginning teacher. You know you are facing a great deal of work and preparation in your new role. Naturally, you are concerned. You want to do a good job. At this point, you could reassure yourself that it will all work out and leave it at that. *Don't.* If you go through the three stages of "creative" worrying—getting information (if you don't know what questions to ask, seek out an experienced teacher), finding information and details of available resources, and making plans and rewarding yourself for doing so—you are far more likely to be "emotionally inoculated" for the first weeks and perhaps the entire first year of teaching, an extremely vulnerable time. Kyriacou and Sutcliffe found that teachers under thirty with zero to four years of experience were more likely to leave teaching than those of any other group.[15] You are also much more likely to be on the path to becoming an effective teacher.

Mental Reprograming

There are a variety of other techniques that can be learned which will enable you to effectively deal with stressors from an attitudinal standpoint. Don't get the impression though, that you can only work through one channel. I am convinced that the R.E.A.D. program must be introduced into your life as a whole, to whatever degree is possible. Just do it gradually. Deep relaxation and aerobic exercise on a regular basis will reduce chronic levels of anxiety and stress in your life. Taking it as it comes will enable you to achieve goals without undue pressure on yourself and others. Then you can learn to deal with specific stressful situations with mental reprograming. This involves two steps: (1) stopping thought and (2) rethinking.

When you find yourself engaged in useless or negative thoughts throughout the teaching day you must first stop them. You can so do by listening to an inner voice that simply yells "stop" or by coupling the command with a visual image of a stop sign. This will give you a momentary pause from enervative modes of thinking so that you can rechannel your processes into the second phase, rethinking.

Rethinking means switching gears to a rational, problem-solving approach. It means not crying over spilled milk, not holding grudges, and getting on with what needs to be done to satisfactorily resolve a problem. Holding grudges is one of the most effective ways to ruin good relationships in a school or classroom. Holding grudges is one way we hang onto the past and let it interfere with what needs to be done.

Imaging

Imaging is another mental reprogramming technique that can help change attitude and awareness. It is simply the name for a *process* of planning, anticipating, or preparing for stressors. However, we usually don't take full advantage of this process native to most of us, and that is when we begin to break down. Imaging is best done on a daily basis, for example, when you are practicing your technique for relaxing. The process involves the following steps:

1. Become aware of the stressors that exist for you *on a daily basis.* On a global level, you should become aware of the major life and job stressors that you experience. You might also want to become more specific and even itemize the stressful incidents in the course of your day.

2. Let the stressors incubate. This stage is very important. Time allows you to be more objective. Some incidents will make you feel embarrassed or angry. This is usually not the time to act.

3. Image helpful strategies during your regular periods of deep relaxation. In the course of a single day, a lot happens to you and you create much of what goes on around you. Demands are constantly being made and

you are "computing" everything on a moment-by-moment basis. Your mind and nervous system are sophisticated biocomputers. The various "programs" you run (thoughts and actions) are different from the "hardware," the body and the nervous system itself. But, there is an intimate relationship between the two. Every event in your daily program has some effect on the hardware, the body. How do we release these effects? How do we unstress the stressors?

The many relaxation techniques are helpful here. In some, where deliberate concentration is not integral to the technique, then a very spontaneous process of imaging can happen on a very subtle level. As a person enjoys the state of deep relaxation, the mind is freewheeling. Much of what has happened during the day can be re-enacted, either in great detail or in a telegraphic fashion. However, in the state of deep relaxation, the emotional charge associated with an incident is harmlessly dissipated. Because the images are mental in nature, the "mental computer" can act extremely rapidly, much more so than a technique such as free association in which a person must verbalize his or her mental impressions. It is much like the difference between telling someone about a dream and the actual dreaming.

If you use a "quiet time" on a regular basis to relax deeply with a method of your choice, your imaging will become a powerful part of your daily routine. Besides becoming more efficient in your actions (you'll find a lot of plans taking place during this time), two important things will start to happen:

- You will "unstress" the stressors in a harmless way. This occurs because your biocomputer will spontaneously allow what was bothering you (and which may have gone "underground") to surface in a harmless way. More of what may bother you on a given day can surface because of the rapidity of mental imagery. You may "forget" some incidents which nevertheless leave their "nervous scar."

  During deep relaxation, these could surface, as well as incidents long forgotten from the past. For this reason alone, using an inside out technique like TM or the relaxation response is probably more effective than an outside in technique which places too much emphasis on the relaxing component. However, once a person becomes adept at an outside in method like progressive relaxation, less effort is needed to relax and more "imaging" occurs.

- As well as releasing stress or, more correctly, the effects of stressors, you will find that your biocomputer will begin to "pop up" solutions to some of the stressors you face. The details of such plans over a period of say, twenty minutes of mental freewheeling, can be very extensive indeed.

This kind of "imaging" is extremely useful. You could find for example, that detailed lesson plans will automatically sequence themselves after a period of incubation. One thing though, you have to put your mind to it. That is, you must first go through the other steps. You have to define the problem and give it time to incubate. Although this kind of imaging can occur outside of quiet time, I think that a regular period of meditation or relaxation on a daily basis maximizes your chances to unstress and image effective and creative ways of dealing with the challenges you face as a teacher.

Diet

The final ingredient in a personal stress management program is diet. Much has been said and written on this topic. Many authors have construed diet as the sole means to a better life, but this cannot be so. However, there is no doubt that a person's diet has a profound effect on his or her mental and physical well-being. The following dietary guidelines are recommended:

- Following Canada's or the U.S.'s dietary guidelines (that is, eating moderately from all the major food groups, and reducing meat and carbohydrate consumption) is the best advice you can get on diet.
- Keeping away from foods with artificial additives (many of which are carcinogenic), flavorings, and colorings is a good idea. Although they are generally present in extremely minute quantities, the average total consumption in the course of a year comes to three pounds! A person can't eat that much poison without being affected in some way. On the other hand, it's an equally bad idea to go hog wild "organic." Many so-called organic foods contain as many pesticides as their commercial counterparts. But if you have the space and inclination to do so, growing some of your own food is highly recommended.
- Avoid liquor and caffeine in excessive doses. Sure, have a few drinks once in a while; it's good for the soul. But don't let it become a primary coping behavior. Caffeine in excess produces symptoms indistinguishable from anxiety neurosis because of its harmful effect on the central nervous system.[16] As a rule of thumb you should drink no more than three to five cups of coffee a day.
- Avoid faddish diets and quick weight loss diets. In the long run, these are generally useless. Long term weight loss is maintained by regular exercise and good eating habits. If you are chronically overweight, you probably require specialized help from a doctor

- or a psychologist who specializes in weight control programs.
- Smoking is dangerous. Avoid it altogether if you possibly can. Don't rely on rationalizations about how your uncle or grandfather lived to be ninety-five even though he smoked. Life is far more complex now. Until science can sift out which factors affect longevity in which way, it's best to be prudent on the side of moderation. But the debate over whether or not smoking is hazardous to your health is over.
- Change some of your eating habits. The North American diet is deteriorating. We consume too much saturated fat, processed sugar, cholesterol, and salt. These have been linked to various diseases including cancer, heart disease, diabetes, and hypertension. As we have seen, we cannot isolate the rising incidence of these diseases from stressors either. Therefore a comprehensive program like R.E.A.D. becomes necessary. In 1974, the U.S. Select Committee on National Nutrition recommended the following changes in American food selection and preparation:[17]

    1. Increase the consumption of fruits, vegetables and whole grains. If overweight, decrease intake and begin exercising.
    2. Decrease consumption of refined and processed sugars.
    3. Decrease consumption of foods high in fats and replace the consumption of saturated fats with fats from vegetable sources. Eat more poultry and fish.
    4. Reduce cholesterol consumption to 300 mg. a day.
    5. Reduce salt intake to about 5 grams a day.

- Finally, I would recommend eating out less often. It's too easy to consume poorly balanced meals that way and you have no control over the quality of ingredients or the methods of preparation.

Summary

There is no research to substantiate the effects of an integrated program like R.E.A.D. on important factors like life expectancy and teaching performance.

The closest we have to this is a study by Dr. Lester Breslow. Over a period of five and a half years, the health habits of 7,000 people were examined. The effect of the following habits were the basis for the study: (1) eight hours sleep every night (depending on individual needs), (2) breakfast every morning, (3) no snacks, (4) maintaining weight within limits, (5) no smoking, (6) moderate alcohol consumption (one drink of hard liquor daily or its equivalent), and (7) moderate exercise.[18] The doctor found:

... that, at age 45, those following six or seven of these habits had an additional life expectancy of 33.1 years, while those at 45 following three or less of the habits had an additional life expectancy of only 21.6 years. That's almost a twelve-year difference in life expectancy at age 45 based on some very simple health habits. Dr. Breslow also found the effect to be cumulative: the more health habits you follow, the better your health.

Remember the following principles:

1. There is no one answer to the problem of teacher stress. Knowledge from a number of fields and a holistic, integrated application of that knowledge in a wide variety of contexts is needed at different times.

2. Stress is inevitable but there is every opportunity to manage it in a productive way. A state of no stress is impossible in nature.

3. Becoming aware of stressors in your personal and teaching life is the first step in managing them.

4. Activity, rest and planning are needed in a balanced way. Anything in excess is never healthy.

5. We *can* change. If we have learned to think and act in certain ways, we can "unlearn" bad habits and develop healthier, more effective methods of thinking, coping, and actualizing. A key attitude is to accept yourself *with your faults*. This means learning to accept who you are, admitting that you can make mistakes (and believing you are allowed to) and carrying on from there in a constructive manner.

6. Just as your students model from your example, you can learn by modeling others.

7. It's never too late. Decide that you care about yourself and others. Decide to live. Start to R.E.A.D. There is no doubt that practicing such a balanced program leads to a healthier professional, personal, and social life. This is the best possible inoculation against personal burnout and a precious personal resource, the value of which is impossible to calculate.

Chapter Eight

Managing Stress in Schools

It's the Principal of the Thing

There are many organizational factors in a school which can be changed or affected to minimize stress. These include (1) principal stress, (2) school climate, (3) working conditions, and (4) preventive stress programs. School climate and stress can be and are shaped in powerful ways by the principal. The principal is the pivot of the school. If he or she beams, so does the school. If he or she stagnates, so does the school. I have seen rusted out schools turn into master schools. I have seen mediocre schools turn into cesspools of community and teacher discontent, *all* as a consequence of the actions of the principal.

The principal leads, directs, and inspires. If the principal is a master administrator, then he or she involves the staff in a process of developing a healthy climate and an exciting learning environment. If the principal is rusted out, then usually staff morale is low. By managing stress effectively, a principal also provides a model of coping for teachers. Both staff and principal feed each other in a cycle that can be either benign or malignant. If all is not well, programs for students become secondary. A rusted out principal often works on the garbage can concept of "keeping the lid on things." Relationships with parents are aloof, if not cold and hostile.

Principals, because of their role, face stressors different from those of teachers. A study completed by the Oregon School Study Council identified the ten most stressful items for administrators as:[1] (1) complying with state, federal, and organizational rules and policies, (2) feeling that meetings take up too much time, (3) trying to complete reports and other paper work on time, (4) trying to gain public approval and financial support for school programs, (5) trying to resolve parent/school conflicts, (6) evaluating staff, (7) having to make decisions affecting individual lives, (8) feeling the work load is too heavy, (9) imposing excessively high self-expectations, and (10) being interrupted frequently by telephone calls.

Two-thirds of the administrators "felt that 70 percent or more of their total life stress resulted from their jobs."[2] In addition to the R.E.A.D. program for managing personal stress then, administrators need to learn to cope with their situations by effective time management and the development of healthier interpersonal relationships. Some suggestions for attitude change were also enumerated in the study and include:[3] approaching problems with an optimistic "I can do it" attitude; sharing problems with spouses and family members; establishing realistic goals that recognize personal limitations and the impossibility of solving all problems; keeping personal emotions out of work; and finally, learning to know yourself and maintaining a sense of humor.

School Climate

School climate may be defined as the fundamental feeling or attitude that pervades a school. It is a composite of teacher, administrator, student, parent, and community attitudes. The climate may be healthy or unhealthy. If unhealthy, then of course everyone's stress is increased.

How can school climate be improved? A penetrating analysis of this problem was published by *Phi Delta Kappan*.[4] The authors of *School Climate Improvement* used Maslow's hierarchy of basic needs in their analysis. They argue that schools must provide for all of the needs on the hierarchy if a wholesome climate is to develop. They also point out that *teacher* needs must be satisfied as well as *student* needs. The authors further state that the universal qualities of trust, respect, caring, high morals, and continuous growth cannot be directly worked on. These are the "higher order" needs on the hierarchy. They feel these needs are satisfied when more specific operations in the school are changed. It is *these* which administrators (and teachers) *can* change. There are program, process, and material determinants of school climate. A general description of each is given in Table 1 on the following page.[5]

The book gives details as to how to rate your school's climate and presents a detailed "how to" description of setting goal priorities and effecting changes in each of the program, process, and material areas.

For example, one of the process determinants is identifying and working with conflicts. Many people believe that schools (and life) should be conflict free. But, "Conflict is not in itself the problem. It becomes

Table 1
School Climate Determinants

Program Determinants	Process Determinants	Material Determinants
Opportunities for active learning	Problem solving ability	Adequate resources
Individualized performance expectations	Improvement of school goals	Supportive and efficient logistical system
Varied learning environments, flexible curriculum and extracurricular activities, support and structure appropriate to learner's maturity	Identifying and working with conflicts	Suitability of school plant
	Effective communications	
	Involvement in decision making; autonomy with accountability	
Rules cooperatively determined	Effective teaching-learning strategies	
Varied reward systems	Ability to plan for for the future	

troublesome when it mounts up, is not faced, and is allowed to fester. In a favorable school climate, conflict is identified and worked on."[6]

If the process of having mechanisms for resolving conflicts is there in the school then it will be visible in many different ways in the major groups that the school serves: principals and other administrators will spend time discussing interpersonal hindrances to team effectiveness; they will feel (and be) competent and confident to deal openly with conflict and will apply conflict management skills when necessary; they will encourage staff, students, and parents to do likewise. As a result, students too will learn conflict management skills. The staff will feel competent in identifying and dealing with conflicts and feel that the administration supports their efforts. They will be able to take their concerns directly to the source rather than verbalizing concerns with friends. Finally, parents will feel that their concerns will be listened to and will seek training for practicing conflict management at home.

Stress researchers have identified a number of characteristics of healthy organizations. The researchers suggest that people who work in them have a significant influence on aspects of their work situation. They feel they are engaged in meaningful and socially important activities and experience a sense of belonging; their needs for self-esteem are satisfied. It is this kind of situation towards which principals must work.

What Teachers Can Do

If your principal doesn't appear to be moving in the direction you feel is needed or if you feel that the teachers need to have a mechanism for communicating their feelings about the school in a positive way, then there is no reason why a group of teachers cannot effect these changes provided everyone is willing to work together.

One of the healthiest things a group of teachers in a school can do is band together for a specific purpose. This can serve two needs: providing an emotional support system and a sounding board for current ideas and feelings among colleagues, and as a means of letting the administration know, in an assertive, nonaggressive way, the teachers' ideas for improving matters. Banding together can take several forms: grade level meetings, coffee klatches, social tete à tetes on Friday nights, weekend retreats and so on. It's vital that a variety of formal and informal means of getting together are arranged. It is also important that the meetings be held on a regular basis and that they not become "bitch sessions." Not that a little bitching is unhealthy, but a lot of it is.

Administrators and teachers (as well as parents) need to work in harmony to improve the school climate. Neither side should feel impositions are being placed on them. Teachers need to feel involved, worthwhile, and needed. They have to share feelings and ideas and be acknowledged for a job well done. A group of teachers can implement changes in school climate as effectively as any administrator provided they win administrative support. But teachers who are gathered together to promote change must also be careful that their presence is viewed in a positive fashion, not in a threatening or destructive one. The group's own climate needs to be continuously evaluated.

Working Conditions

Working conditions in a school covers two aspects: (1) classroom, timetables, and curriculum, and (2) salary and benefits. Whenever studies of teacher satisfaction are carried out, it is interesting that, in general, the majority of teachers claim to be satisfied with their classroom conditions and with salaries. Needs other than economic ones are often ranked before salary in such studies.

However, those teachers who are feeling burned out (an average of

25 percent at any given time), and wish to get out of the profession, poor salary, poor promotion prospects, and general dissatisfaction are given as the reasons.[7] Perhaps we need to examine whether teachers are answering such questionnaires in "socially desirable" ways. But we also need to examine very closely the organizational variables involved in teacher burnout and job satisfaction.

One theorist makes what I think is an important contribution to thinking in this area. Frederick Herzberg feels we should stop thinking of satisfaction and dissatisfaction as opposite ends of the same continuum.[8] He feels there are *intrinsic* and *extrinsic* factors that are two completely separate dimensions of job satisfaction. Extrinsic factors include such things as inadequate pay, incompetent supervision, noisy working conditions and the like while intrinsic factors include a sense of achievement, accomplishment, responsibility, and challenge. Dissatisfaction is seen, therefore, as a product of the work environment and satisfaction as a function of the content of work.

Research showing a low (but significant) correlation between teacher stress and satisfaction and other studies seem to support Herzberg's two factor theory. The value of this analysis is evident when we begin to apply it. For instance, customary administrative and trustee moves to affect teacher motivation include evaluations, in-services, setting the hours a teacher is to be at school, and so on. These policies must be carefully determined and administered. If not, they can often make matters worse by widening the gap between teachers, administrators, and trustees. I don't mean that evaluations and in-services should stop, but only that they be seen in perspective and handled thoughtfully. If we are to make any inroads in affecting teacher motivation, then the previous suggestions regarding changing school climate are far more important, simply because they are more closely connected with the heart of teacher satisfaction. The intrinsic factors regarding teacher motivation are governed by a set of values. These of course are closely tied to the values of the community. Therefore, rather than frequently having workshops and professional development sessions for teachers, it's probably more useful to occasionally have a Community Teacher Day. "Workshops designed to clarify community and teacher value systems might be a most effective tool in reducing community conflicts and tensions by effecting changes in both teacher and parental behavior and in reconciling what may only appear (perhaps as a result of poor communication) to be differences in value systems."[9] We are now in a position, using Herzberg's two factor theory, to discuss some other organizational suggestions regarding the alleviation of teacher burnout.

Intrinsic Factors: These should <u>increase</u> teacher satisfaction.

1. Seek to improve your own teaching skills. Since, for the most

part, teachers who feel burned out also feel they are no longer making a difference with their students, then it is urgent that you see that *you* must make the changes yourself. It is vital that you see that you *do* make a difference in children's lives and that you *can* control or improve on this in yourself and in your classroom.

2. Learn to become open and to share feelings with students and colleagues. You may be quite surprised at how receptive others will be when dealt with in this way.
3. Extend the freedom you enjoy in making curriculum choices. Develop themes and lessons based on them. If you do not enjoy freedom of choice in curriculum areas, seek positive ways of changing this.
4. Change your classroom conditions. Sometimes just rearranging the furniture helps.
5. Create ways of teaching the "basics" but if you are always changing things, take a rest and evaluate the effectiveness of what you are doing.
6. Work toward expanding your professional growth. Structured breaks from teaching can be very helpful and sabbatical leave is a powerful tool for accomplishing many objectives related to professional growth. Unfortunately, sabbatical leaves are not a routine part of a teacher's job; they are granted only with permission. Perhaps they should be automatically granted every seven or eight years for all teachers. Financially, this could be accomplished by nominal monthly pay deductions for that purpose. Regular sabbaticals would broaden professional and personal growth, provide a rest from classroom stressors, and perhaps provide an honorable exit for those whose talents lie in areas other than teaching.

Extrinsic Factors: These should <u>decrease</u> teacher dissatisfaction.

1. Accept and praise your administrators for jobs well done. If your administrator does not do a good job, begin a healthy process of seeking change.
2. Write letters to the editor of your local newspaper, but don't be negative. Just point out what you see as being good in your school system.
3. Strive to close the gap between home and school. A values clarification workshop by an expert in the area could be extremely useful. Take part in dialogues and workshops with your local board members. They are always willing to listen. But let them know good things too. If you disagree with their views, let them know why in a diplomatic way. If you don't know how to be

diplomatic, don't say anything until you've taken a course in assertiveness training.

Preventive Stress Programs

Should any principal wish to effect an organizational change having immediate impact, then a R.E.A.D. program should be introduced. The program must of course be voluntary in nature, but it should include all four components of deep relaxation, exercise, attitude, and diet.

Resources for such a program will vary from school system to school system and thus affect the feasibility of implementation. Most large systems have school psychologists. Surely if we can refer students to psychologists for help, then some can be freed and trained to deal more specifically with managing teacher stress.

They could in fact train counselors to do likewise. Since most schools also have counselors, then most schools could also eventually have "stress consultants" for the teaching staff.

If a school system were to implement such programs, then other facets could gradually be introduced such as:

- screening (on site) for hypertension
- alcoholism and drug counselling
- personal counseling and therapy
- nutritional information
- stop smoking programs
- monitoring of progressive diseases
- assertiveness training
- interpersonal communication skills
- time management training

These programs and others would greatly enhance teacher effectiveness, personal health, and job satisfaction. Absenteeism due to stress related illness should decrease. The cost of absenteeism alone is staggering. Albrecht estimates that stress related occurrences such as absenteeism, turnover, overstaffing as a consequence of poor job performance, and antisocial acts directed against a company (for example, theft and deliberate waste) cost America a staggering $150 billion annually.[10] With over 22 million teachers in the work force, the cost of teacher stress is some $3.5 billion annually. And these are conservative estimates. It's true that we cannot eliminate all these factors, even with good stress management programs. But we *can* make a significant dent in what is surely a subtle, damaging, and dangerous contemporary phenomenon.

There is no easy solution to the problem of organizational stressors affecting burnout. The above suggestions are, in my view, only temporary measures which might bring some relief. Certainly they are necessary and vital, particularly given the situation as it presently exists. But the deeper reasons for burnout, particularly teacher selection, training, and follow-through and public control over education will continue to plague the organization of schools and perpetuate the burnout problem unless bold and positive countermeasures are taken.

Chapter Nine

Managing Classroom Stressors

The teacher is the most important part of any classroom, and vital in the learning process. A teacher opens, encourages, leads, and inspires the educational welfare of students. Since education is universal, teachers not only create the classroom—in effect, they contribute to the creation of society itself.

The master teacher, the rust-out, and the chronically miserable all relate to stress, pressure, and change in different ways. It should be obvious that one cannot eliminate stress or pressure totally. To do so would be disastrous. *Some* pressure is necessary to maintain productivity. *Too much* pressure results in burnout. *Too little* pressure results in rustout. The optimal level of pressure, which is different for every person, must be maintained in a reasonable balance in order to maintain both productivity and job satisfaction.

Just as a manager or foreman must know his men in order to maximize performance from each one, so too must a superintendent know his principals, principals know their teachers, and teachers know their students and themselves. Trying to apply the same pressure to all will create too little or too much stress and may make matters worse rather than better.

Master teachers, without some kind of professional refreshment at intervals, burn out eventually. The chronically miserable require professional counseling. Rustouts need more pressure. To change this situation and improve the quality of education requires an honest appraisal of where one fits on the scale. If you are still deriving a great deal of satisfaction from your job and believe you will remain a teacher for the balance of your career, then get in there and fight for the changes, both internal and external, necessary for improving education for future generations.

If you are a rustout and find yourself unwilling to change, then you should seriously consider an occupation that demands more initiative. But if you *are* willing to change, take the initiative to do so. You will most certainly find satisfaction.

For those who are chronically miserable, perhaps early retirement or a change to an occupation requiring little interaction with people would be best for all concerned. In any case, don't be afraid to seek professional advice. The problem and its ramifications for teachers and students alike is *very* serious. A less stressful society is an urgent priority, and education can be a tool for shaping it.

R.E.A.D.I.E.

The components of an effectively managed classroom which prepares students for the future includes those elements already discussed for teacher stress management and one other component—individualized education (I.E.). It would not be difficult for teachers to introduce two ten-minute sessions of deep relaxation for students daily. Nor would it be difficult to introduce a daily ten-minute cardiovascular fitness exercise program.[1] It would be more difficult, but not impossible, to modify the student's diet. And finally, it is vital that educators become much more adept in identifying and encouraging individual talents and abilities. A comprehensive, holistic program like R.E.A.D.I.E. could have profound effects.

Relaxation and Learning

Because deep relaxation is an essential component of stress management and stress directly affects so much of our lives, it is disturbing that so little research exists on the effects of deep relaxation on learning in children. Some evidence has come to light that certain techniques can affect certain aspects of the learning process, but this research was done on adults, not children. However, relaxation has been used successfully in treating such stress related disorders in children as insomnia, asthma, test anxiety, excitable behavior in psychotic children, and hyperactivity.[2] There is some evidence that deep relaxation, in conjunction with other psychological techniques, is extremely useful in educational settings.

Counselors and teachers can work to bring these benefits to students by implementing periods of "quiet time" prior to the beginning of the school day and once again near the end of the school day. You will be doing yourself and your students a great service by implementing this practice. Students in all grades experience some degree of tension at one time or another. Children can be worried about friends, or be under pressure to succeed, to always be right, to have approval, and so on. These kinds of feelings and experiences are too often repressed or never discussed in schools.

Regular periods of relaxation can help reduce these feelings of tension, those knots and butterflies in the stomach. Once children learn the skills, they can relax without specific directions from you. And as you become more adept at teaching them, you can then become more helpful in dealing with the specific problem areas each student has.

If introducing these techniques to your students seems uncomfortably innovative to your school system, discuss the matter with the administration. If your school has a guidance counselor or school psychologist, he or she is the ideal resource person. Counselors should be able to deal with individuals or small groups should the need arise for more intensive work beyond the classroom. For example, some youngsters are extremely restless and may require a modified approach which sequences the relaxation skills into smaller "bits" than what you could do in the classroom.

If you decide to implement a relaxation program, you should prepare your class beforehand by discussing tension, how it manifests and is experienced and how it can be dealt with. (Your students will provide you with plenty of examples from their own experiences.) You can then suggest that you feel the class should learn how to deal with anxiety and tension. The first step will be for everyone to learn how to relax.

If your students are very young (grade one), then you will want to read the *Turtle Manual*.[3] "Doing turtle" simply means the child "draws in" his body, much like a turtle does when faced with a threatening situation. The turtle technique is aimed specifically at helping youngsters learn to deal with aggressive and impulsive feelings, but the method can easily be adapted to your particular needs as well because a relaxation technique is included in the manual.

Next, find a script or sequence for teaching students how to relax. You can modify the adult progressive relaxation version given in Appendix C or you can use the script in Appendix D for this purpose. Practice it beforehand with one or two students. In fact, if one student becomes good at it, he or she can serve as a "demonstration model," freeing you to give instructions to the others. Having a child model will also tend to inhibit the embarrassment some children have when tensing and relaxing certain muscle groups, especially those of the nose, eyes, and face. You should ignore the giggling, tell them it's part of the procedure and continue. Persistently annoying or disruptive students should have one-to-one sessions with the counselor or school psychologist.

The use of "guided imagery" can be helpful in this regard: see for example, the puppet and balloon images given in Appendix C. Some teachers have gone well beyond that with their students and use guided fantasies.[4] I do not recommend any form of these inside out procedures until a teacher feels truly expert at dealing with the kinds of experiences students have with outside in sessions.

In introducing outside in technique to students, begin with no more than three muscle groups per day. After your students become skilled and you have dealt with individual problems, you can devote later sessions to work in other areas, particularly social skills.

Exercise

There is a paucity of evidence relating exercise to the efficiency of cognitive functioning. Exercise in most schools is generally viewed as part of the physical education program, not as part of life outside the P.E. class. This sad state of affairs developed from the specialization of school curricula and the low regard we have in our society for physical fitness in general. It is vital that good exercise habits be established early in life. For this to occur, students need to see good models from teachers themselves.

We also should not adapt a policy of laissez faire regarding student choice. If students are allowed to opt out of an exercise program, the ones who do so are generally the ones who need it most.

Besides what happens in physical education classes, students are rarely expected to exercise in school. And for some, physical education is not available even if they desire it because it often isn't offered, particularly at the high school level.

Specific programs and exercises to develop cardiovascular fitness and to prepare students for healthier, longer lives could be developed by physical education instructors for use in all classrooms outside of the formal physical education periods.

Attitude

Development of healthy, stress-coping attitudes in children is a neglected area in our educational system. To introduce such skills requires the conviction that there is much of importance beyond the basics. Perhaps learning to read people is as important as learning to read. Many affective programs are now being introduced informally in many schools. Magic Circle is one example.[5] However, I do not advocate rigidly adhering to any kit, system, or technique. These are just time savers. Expose yourself to a variety of kits, ideas, and points of view and develop your own programs with well-defined objectives for the students.

These programs must exist as the third essential ingredient in preparing for the future. There are many components and related issues in the development of healthy attitudes and self-concept. They all relate to effective stress management in the classroom.

Communication: The Heart of Teaching

A major component in successful teaching lies in the ability to communicate effectively. By communication, I mean the process of interpreting information from the teaching environment and making optimum responses to one's students and colleagues. The process varies, of course, from situation to situation, but it rests on a few solid principles:

- Accept yourself. To be an effective communicator, you must be comfortable with yourself as a person. A self-actualizing person not only has a high self-regard for his or her strengths but is able to accept some weaknesses without feeling guilty or less worthy as a human being. If you can accept yourself, you will go a long way toward accepting others.
- Learn to listen. Listening is a delicate (and very nearly lost) art. Students often try to reach out even through negative actions. It's essential that a teacher learn to interpret this information in a way that is not threatening. It's not easy to determine whether problems in the classroom are the result of the teacher's stress or inefficiency, or something that lies in the child or in his home. The situation is usually complex. Nothing comes of trying to find someone or something to blame. Every effort should be exerted for the sake of the child.

    A sensible strategy is simply to define the problem, accept it temporarily and seek ways to resolve it as reasonably as possible. Some problems lie beyond the scope of any one individual, so outside resources such as consultants, psychologists, reading specialists, school counselors, and so on should be used without fear that it reflects somehow on one's own competence. If the situation is truly one where you have contributed to the problem, seek ways of changing your own behavior—without self-retribution.
- Respond in a way that shows you listened. Students at any age need to know you respect and accept them for what they are. That doesn't mean you have to like them all, but it does mean that you won't belittle them even if you don't like them. The fact that a teacher respects his or her students is communicated in many, often small, ways. A teacher must *earn* the respect of his students. Respect doesn't come automatically merely because the teacher is in a position of authority and expects respect as a result. If you are interested in developing more effective skills in listening and communication, research shows that this is something that can be both learned and maintained by teachers.[6]

Problem Solving

In this context, problem solving refers to *social* problem solving.

Once your students become more experienced at relaxing, you will probably want to introduce versions of imaging with them. With imaging one can deal with very specific and individual problems. Problem solving strategies using cognitive-behavioral methods are developing rapidly in North America, particularly for use in the treatment of hyperactivity and impulsivity. Several programs are now available.[7]

The purpose of these techniques is to teach children alternatives to the nonproductive ways they usually develop for dealing with problem situations. This is done through a sequence of (1) defining the problem, (2) generating alternatives, (3) modeling the alternatives, and then (4) giving children the opportunity to practice them in such a way that they receive feedback. This sequence can be expanded to include classroom meetings to discuss other areas of concern. William Glasser recommends the regular use of classroom meetings to help teachers and students evaluate feelings and behavior.[8] He describes three kinds of meetings: (1) social problem-solving meetings, which concern themselves with the students' behavior in school, (2) open-ended meetings which concern themselves with thought provoking questions, and (3) educational-diagnostic meetings which deal with how well students understand curriculum concepts. A teacher may use any one or a combination of any of the above kinds of meetings to help students. The usefulness of this approach has recently been documented.[9]

Fate Control

This intriguing juxtaposition of terms is used by Mary Budd Rowe in her work with locus of control.[10] It is important in dealing with stress that a person have the feeling that she or he is in control of what happens.

Some children feel that what they do has no effect whatsoever on their marks or whether or not they receive praise from the teacher. If this is true of a student, then traditional means of reinforcement, such as verbal praise, will have little effect on such a pupil. These children might feel that life is like a game of craps—they believe, probably without knowing exactly why, that there is no reliable means for improving the odds in their favor.

Students who subscribe to the bowler perception of the world on the other hand, believe that results *can* be affected by one's behavior, much like one's bowling game can be improved by refining all the physical movements involved. These students probably have more chance of having their self-concept damaged as a result of failure at a task because they blame themselves. The "craps" orientation on the other hand, protects the individual's self-concept in that it is kept in a perpetually low posture. But the behavior of students with a bowler orientation can be more easily modified by appropriate feedback. Are your students bowlers or crappers? Budd Rowe gives some guidelines for helping students develop a sense of fate control. Some of these are:[11]

1. Select tasks where the quality of the outcome can be judged by the student.
2. Use "wait time" in discussions. Research shows that teachers usually don't allow sufficient time for students to respond when they are asked a question. If the student doesn't respond quickly, teachers will generally either ask another question or another student. The average wait time between questions is 1.5 seconds. If teachers increase this wait time to four seconds, then creative, productive responses increase in the class. This simple increase in wait time allows students to process the question and generate alternatives.
3. Reduce the number of overt verbal rewards and punishments. This allows the development of an environment where individuals can learn "fate control."
4. Encourage speculation by asking questions with a range of answers, possibilities, and interpretations.
5. Teach students to ask questions. Hold "ask me" sessions.
6. Involve the students in setting goals and goal assessment.

Discipline and Motivation

Probably no topic other than lesson preparation receives more teacher attention than discipline and its close relative, motivation. You cannot discuss one without the other.

Consider the difficulty of controlling a large group such as a room full of youngsters. Intense feelings, particularly negative ones, can be generated continually. The situation can become volatile very quickly. It's no wonder that class control is a matter of concern to all teachers and a source of great stress for some.

But it is difficult, particularly for older, more experienced teachers, to discuss the subject. Student novice teachers are justifiably concerned about discipline and are given much in the way of advice and assistance. This is generally not so for the experienced teacher, who expects or is expected to have classroom control at all times. Many teachers learn to keep their classes quiet, but this just might be the "garbage can" approach. If a teacher expects perfect control, it is difficult to discuss the topic with anyone. Anxiety could increase. The stress and exhaustion a teacher feels at the end of the day is closely linked to the effort required to "keep discipline."

Effective classroom management techniques are therefore crucial to the management of teacher stress. The art of teaching includes the ability to keep motivation and rewards (or punishments) at an optimal level. Therefore "discipline" in a special education class might be (and usually is) quite different than in a regular classroom. The underlying principles are often the same however.

Motivation

I would like to discuss the two types of motivation, intrinsic and extrinsic. The basis for this dichotomy is made on the grounds of the source of information that is required in order to maintain the behavior. For instance, if the information is required to maintain or enlarge what is already "programmed" into the individual, then the source is "internal." Motivation is easy to maintain in these circumstances. The teacher simply ensures that the source of information is adequate to what the student already knows. Adequate information, in turn, means that a task is neither too easy nor too difficult for a student. For example, a learning-disabled student with no basis for dealing with abstract math is dealing with a task that is irrelevant to his or her existing knowledge. The child, therefore, won't do the task. On the other hand, if new information is perfectly congruent with existing knowledge, then nothing new is added. This kind of task will be boring to the student. If the student does it at all, it will be for some extrinsic reason (a tangible or intangible reward or fear of punishment or repercussion).

Master teachers already know this. They realize that providing tasks irrelevant to the child's needs, or continually punishing a child for not working or bribing a child to do good work are not necessarily effective ways to aid learning. They strive to make their lessons interesting and to individualize instruction for all students as much as possible. Ideally, all learning in a classroom should be intrinsic and positive. Unfortunately, this is not possible at the present time. The main reason is simply the lack of time. A teacher cannot under current conditions, prepare individual lessons for each child nor can a teacher always perfectly match what a student already knows and what he or she needs to know.

Disregarding for the moment the placement in the regular classroom of truly handicapped students, it is possible to individualize instruction to some extent without inordinate amounts of work for the teacher. It does mean *some* extra work but once you begin, you will be well rewarded when you see the increased interest and motivation in your students. The sequence is quite straightforward.

First, know your students well. This means you should have a good idea of their abilities and achievement levels. You should have some clear picture of their home environment and any special needs the student might have. This kind of information is available from parents, other teachers (be careful however of "labeling"), counselors, cumulative records, standardized tests and the like. This is where the most time comes in—gathering the information and getting a clear picture of each student.

Next, individualize within the same lesson. This means you prepare the *same* lesson for the class, but because of your knowledge of the student, you are able to enrich or to remediate as the case might be. This means setting different objectives for each subgroup. This does *not* mean that you put the same students into an enrichment or remediation group and leave them there for the year. It *does* mean creating flexible groupings which could change from week to week, or even day to day depending on the needs of the class. For instance, just because a student is very bright does not mean he or she has all the knowledge necessary to deal with a particular math skill. For a week, that student might have to be in with a group of slower students for some drills in division or multiplication or whatever the case might be. If you know what your students need, you can make arrangements for outside help from parent volunteers or student assistants. You can also use peer tutoring in the classroom. Or you can get older students who have difficulty with, say, reading, to help younger students having difficulty with the same skill. Both students profit from such an arrangement. If you know how to delegate responsibility, you can get a lot accomplished without burdening yourself.

Finally, keep accurate and ongoing records. This requires an accurate assessment of the scope and sequence of the subjects you are teaching. You will need to know where your students are within each skill area for each subject and group them accordingly. You will have to have a variety of materials available and you will need to become flexible and adaptable. Above all, you will need to be in complete control of your educational plans. Needless to say, if you have not attempted this kind of thing before you may need some help for a while from local consultants.

Because many teachers are geared to teaching the "average" child, effective methods for classroom management are not always possible. A teacher may reach for an immediate solution to a problem, which may bring temporary relief in the short run, but does nothing in the long run.

Many feel that teachers are "too soft" on students; they should be made to "toe the line." Usually, this implies using some form of punishment or failing more students for not meeting the standards of the subject taught. I am not opposed to the occasional use of these methods of extrinsic motivation. Students who are already well socialized maintain acceptable behavior in order to avoid punishment.

The mistake comes in applying this principle to *all* students, particularly those who are chronic behavior problems. I have often seen students, for example, who were at the principal's office for their daily nagging for unreasonably extended periods of time—months and sometimes even years. No one seemed to have tried alternative disciplinary methods. In days gone by, such students simply left the system when they were old enough (many still do). Fortunately, there is now more emphasis being placed on educational opportunity for all. If this is to become a reality, then all school systems must begin building genuine alternatives for the variety of needs that students have. Such alternatives cannot possibly work however, if punishment is the prime motivator. Students who are chronic behavior problems can often learn acceptable behaviors through effective use of positive extrinsic motivation and patient handling. Once the correct behaviors are learned, and the student is doing things in acceptable ways because she or he wants to, the extrinsic motivators can be gradually "faded."

In other instances, students who are chronic behavior problems in regular academic settings can become model students in an environment where more courses are geared to their needs and interests. The development and extension of special educational services and an extended curriculum is therefore of the utmost importance.

The bottom line for some students is removal from school. The reasons for this were discussed earlier. Sometimes it *is* best that a student be expelled from school and allowed to experience the consequences of his or her own actions. Such students frequently return to school at a later date much more willing to learn.

Diet

Research at the University of Cincinnati has recently uncovered what has been suspected by those aware of North America's dangerous stress levels. It has been found that some children have dangerously high elevations of certain fatty substances in their blood. This makes them likely candidates for heart disease thirty or forty years down the road.[12] These same students stuff themselves with fattening foods and eat excessive amounts of cholesterol and saturated fats.

Diet has also been implicated in hyperactivity.[13] The research is not as strong as the hypothesis but some recent work has indeed shown certain behaviors and learning performance to be affected by the addition of certain foods or food additives to the diet.[14]

The U.S. dietary goals discussed earlier once more come to mind. Students need to be educated as to what constitutes a wholesome diet and what doesn't, and to be encouraged to eat sensibly.

Pacing

Allowing students to progress at their own rate is important. Teachers should allow students' output to maximize by not putting on too much or too little pressure. This also implies that a good teacher, like a good foreman, knows what "too much" or "too little" is for each child. It also requires recognition on everyone's part that "optimum output" for each child varies. Too many North Americans are caught in the debilitating expectation that all children must read by age six. Beginning teachers especially begin to panic when they inevitably discover that a certain subgroup of their class is just not responding. There is tremendous pressure from many corners to bring each child to "grade level" in every subject area. This can sometimes occur provided a lot of "ifs" are satisfied. The implementation of PL 94-142 is an attempt to make all those "ifs" possible for all handicapped students.

There is no doubt that special education services are extremely vital for many children. The necessity of writing IEPs, the whole concept of "due process" and the addition of millions of dollars into school systems to provide psychologists, resource teachers, and special materials, will indeed help thousands of children if the spirit of the law is carried out. But we are still left with the nagging and fundamental problem of trying to equalize what is basically unequal. Providing equal opportunity means trying to eradicate those factors associated with lack of academic success. These include socioeconomic status and deficits in language development and a hundred other factors as well. As much as we need to improve those deficits in children where they exist, we need, I feel, to do something more. We need to extend our current curriculum to include the concept of "multiple talents." We need to realize that *every* child is potentially gifted.

Multiple Talents

If we examine almost any North American classroom today, we will find that the primary focus is academic. Oh, we pay lip service to the concept of developing the "whole child," perhaps by adding art and music to the core subjects, but by and large, the system is quite narrow. Since academic subjects are so unduly emphasized, only a certain number of students can excel. We have set up a very competitive system whereby those students who are academically inclined and whose background supports it, are put "through the hoops." The ones who make it are allowed to continue with higher education, and a smaller number still get into graduate school. Education is the golden key to upward social mobility, but only for a select few.

Many of those who made it through this system became teachers. And like it or not, they perpetuate the same "straight and narrow" path. Those students who toe the academic line are rewarded. Those who do not are either overtly punished or put in a situation of "no growth." Any dormant capacities or talents they might have are simply not cultivated by an academic system in which an instructor, quite removed from his students, attempts to pour knowledge into vessels who then receive and regurgitate it back to him. This isn't education.

It's true that teachers don't *mean* to be like that, but by and large they are trained to do just that. And it is our very narrow conception of education that forces it upon them. For example, the psychologist J. R. Guilford has identified some 120 components of human intellect.[15] There are five "thinking operations" he has identified as one important dimension.

These five are (1) cognition, (2) memory, (3) divergent thinking (creative, "more than one possible solution" type of thinking), (4) convergent thinking (logical, "one right answer" type of thinking), and (5) evaluation.

Researchers observed the amount of time a typical teacher spends cultivating these operations in children; this is what they found:[16] 26% of the teachers' time was devoted to developing cognition, 33% on memory, 3% on divergent thinking, 4% on convergent production, and 5% on evaluation. A staggering 30% of classroom time was spent on what the researchers called "routine" operations related to classroom maintenance—which had nothing to do with thinking or learning.

When asked to rate how much time these same teachers thought they were spending cultivating each of the areas, they estimated they were spending 30% of their time on cognition, 28% on memory, 12% on divergent thinking, 14% on convergent thinking, and 16% on evaluation. They were also asked to rate what the ideal amount of time should be on each area. These figures are listed in Table 2.

There is tremendous discrepancy between what we do in classrooms and what we say we do. Fortunately, this can change. When these same teachers were shown how to "brainstorm" (a procedure requiring all five mental operations), and shown how to apply brainstorming to their classrooms, a post-evaluation after just six weeks showed a significant change in the amount of time teachers devoted to each area. The ratios more closely approximated the ideal times they had set previously. These figures are also shown in Table 2.[17]

Table 2

	Time Spent on Thinking Operations			
	Observed Baseline	Teacher Estimates	Teacher Ideal	Post-Training Observed Time
Cognition	26	30	21	20
Memory	33	28	18	21
Divergent Production	3	12	23	18
Convergent Production	4	14	20	16
Evaluation	5	16	18	16
Routine	30	—	—	9

The interesting thing about this project was that the teachers were completely unaware of the routine category. But by learning only a simple technique, these teachers found that the students were much more interested in their work, were motivated, and were more independent. They could settle down and do their work much easier.

But that is only the tip of the iceberg. Dr. Calvin Taylor, a pioneer in the area of multiple talent curriculum, says there are more than eighty talents we can currently identify and teach. The "Taylor Talent Totem Pole" in Figure 3 illustrates this idea best. The totem pole is a simple way of explaining how almost all students can be encouraged to develop their latent talents.

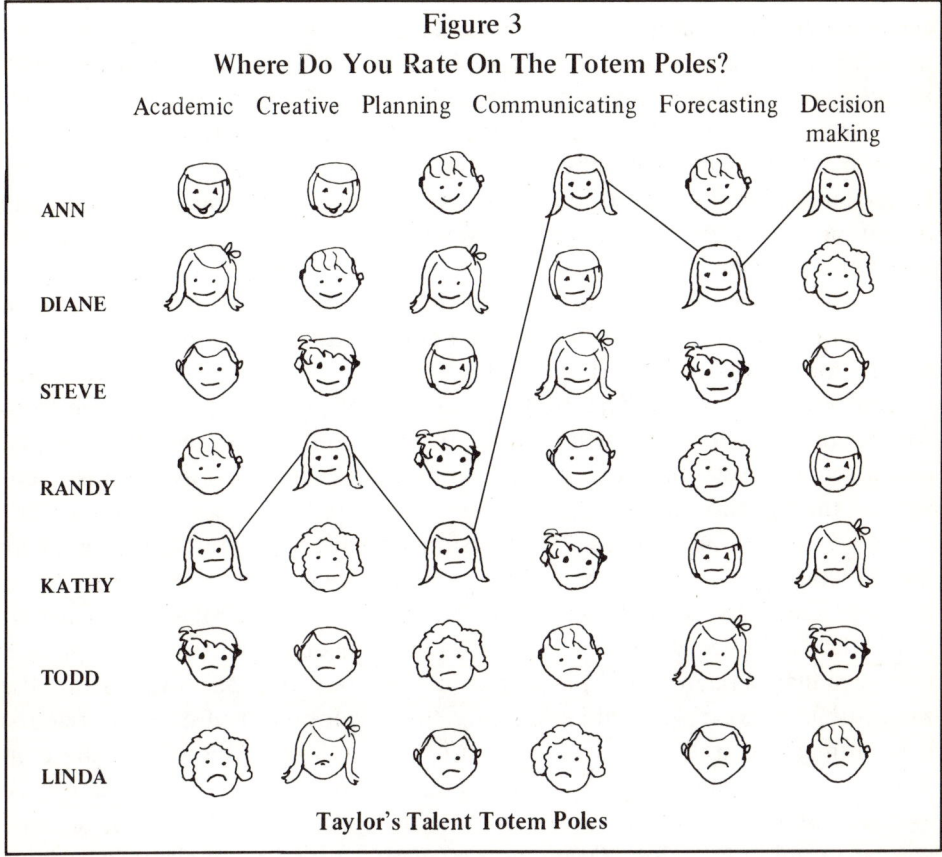

In our current system, Ann, Diane, Steve, and perhaps Randy would be considered outstanding students. The sad truth is that these same four students would likely not change very much in their ranking over the years. There may be a few late academic bloomers, but by and large students who enjoy early success in school maintain it.

Suppose, however, that we add some other important talent areas such as creativity, planning, communicating, forecasting, and decision making. You can see, by following any one of the students, that sooner or later their particular cognitive skill would come to the fore. In Figure 3, we see Kathy finally achieving a top of the class status when communication and decision making are encouraged. If we encourage just ten talent areas (and remember there are many more), then half of all students will score above the 90th percentile in one of these areas. By extending the number of talent areas, then of course the probability of encouraging each student's latent capabilities increases.

These many cognitive areas *must* be developed in students. The best kept secret in education today is that there is virtually *no correlation* between success in school, as measured by academic grades, and later success in life, by whatever criteria you wish to measure success.[19] A student who is lacking academically may never become a successful surgeon because she or he won't get into medical school in the first place. But that student may go on to become a success in business or many other areas requiring the use of talents and skills not encouraged in school. By the same token, the successful surgeon is not necessarily the one who had good grades in medical school. Other talents besides those taught in universities are obviously required and it is *these* which any MD or PhD must still learn after she or he has acquired a higher education.

In a report to the U.S. Office of Education, Taylor says it is most important that we identify (1) all the nation's known human resources and the degree to which current curricula develop them, (2) the degree to which current scientific research is used in educational programs, (3) the degree to which education relates to the world of work, and (4) the degree to which educational programs help people develop greater self-awareness, self-understanding, and insight.

Taylor points out that teachers might achieve greater status by giving greater status to the student (where it belongs anyway). How is this to be accomplished? By what he calls the "double-barreled curriculum." Current curricula emphasize *content* in the different subject areas. As a consequence, only academic talents are promoted. By encouraging *process,* within the same subject areas, we would encourage the development of multiple talents. Communication and creativity obviously are two processes within the content area of language arts while decision making and forecasting could be encouraged in the area of mathematics. More details of this whole scheme can be found in his book, *Teaching for Talents and Gifts.* Teachers who have attended his workshops have comments like:[20]

> I've learned that children can be stars as often as the teacher will allow, that gifted students do not perform highly in all areas, and that the "talents approach" can be just as beneficial to the low-achieving student.

And:

> I want to develop in my students the ability to think, not just babble what I have babbled to them. I will let my students have productive thinking processes which come naturally. I will implement by devel-

oping specific talents, using subject matter as fodder and I can do this by changing current learning centers to "function junctions."

There are encouraging signs that this double-barreled approach is being implemented in certain states and provinces. But on the whole, Taylor's ideas about developing talent are largely in the earliest stages. I am aware of no programs in Canada attempting this kind of work and in the U.S., only a very few classrooms in each of about forty states have a multiple talent project.

This kind of individualized curriculum is an idea whose time has come. To be most effective, we must still incorporate the other components of stress management discussed in this book. A sensible program of deep relaxation, regular exercise, healthy attitude, and diet offers relief for many contemporary stress problems. That program plus an individualized education program that develops the many facets of thinking necessary in our incredibly complex society would truly help us be ready for the future.

Conclusion

Some symptoms of burnout affect probably more than 90 percent of all teachers. About 25 percent of the teaching profession finds their jobs "very stressful" and many more are unlikely to remain in their work.

Teacher stress and burnout is a complex subject. The sources of stress are many and stem from historical sources, current training and selection procedures, current expectations about the role of education, and life and job demands and changes. Solutions to the problem are not to be found in any one method or way. Stress management must be multipronged and simultaneously applied in many areas and must include at least the four areas discussed in the R.E.A.D. program. For students, the additional component of individualized education must also be added.

Managing personal and teaching stressors effectively allows you to achieve more of your potential as a teacher and as a human being. The ultimate responsibility for this lies with you. You can control the events of your life. I leave you with this advice:

- Take it easy. Take it as it comes.
- If it doesn't come, go out and get it.
- If it's still not there, create it.
- Do what you need to do. It is *never* too late.

Appendix A

Please fill the questionnaires out in these Appendices to the best of your ability. You should choose the ones you wish to do and complete them before reading the interpretations.

Life Stress Scale I

Life Event	Mean Value
1. Death of a spouse	100
2. Divorce	73
3. Marital separation	65
4. Jail term	63
5. Death of close family member	63
6. Personal injury or illness	53
7. Marriage	50
8. Fired at work	47
9. Marital reconciliation	45
10. Retirement	45
11. Change in health of family member	44
12. Pregnancy	40
13. Sex difficulties	39
14. A new member in the family	39
15. Business readjustment	39
16. Change in financial state	38
17. Death of a close friend	37
18. Change to different line of work	36
19. Change in number of arguments with spouse	35
20. Mortgage of $40,000	31
21. Foreclosure of mortgage or loan	30
22. Change in responsibilities at work	29
23. Son or daughter leaving home	29
24. Trouble with in-laws	29
25. Outstanding personal achievement	28
26. Wife beginning or stopping work	26
27. Beginning or ending school	26
28. Change in living conditions	25
29. Revision of personal habits	24
30. Trouble with boss	23
31. Change in work hours or conditions	20
32. Change in residence	20
33. Change in schools	20
34. Change in recreation	19
35. Change in church activities	19
36. Change in social activities	19
37. Mortgage or loan less than $10,000	17
38. Change in sleeping habits	16
39. Change in number of family gatherings	15
40. Change in eating habits	15
41. Vacation	13
42. Christmas	12
43. Minor violations of the law	11

Interpretation:

L.C.U. Magnitude Scale	
Mild crisis	150-199
Moderate crisis	200-299
Major crisis	300+

Life Stress Scale II
(Hough, Fairbank, and Garcia Adaptation)

Life Event	Mean Value	Life Event	Mean Value
1. Death of spouse	190	33. Frequent minor illnesses	53
2. Mental illness	142	34. Birth of second or later child	52
3. Divorce	137	35. Move over 1,000 miles	52
4. Racial intermarriage	116	36. Trouble with boss	52
5. Marital separation	115	37. Marriage	50
6. Death of close family member	111	38. Wife stops work	50
7. Fired at work	101	39. Begin school	48
8. Jail term	99	40. Wife begins work	46
9. Personal injury or illness	91	41. Engaged	46
10. Sex difficulties	90	42. Change in responsibilities at work	45
11. Pregnancy	89	43. End school	45
12. Marked decrease in income	88	44. Move out of city or area to within 1,000 miles	43
13. Law suit	85	45. Problems in school	42
14. Change in number of arguments with spouse	135	46. Trouble with friends	40
15. Marital reconciliation	85	47. Mortgage or loan less than $10,000	38
16. Foreclosure of mortgage or loan	83	48. Change in work hours or conditions	36
17. Failure at school or training school	82	49. Change in sleeping habits	36
18. Birth of first child	78	50. Change in social activities	35
19. Health of family member becomes worse	77	51. Marked increase in income	35
20. Death of close friend	77	52. Change in eating habits	33
21. Son or daughter leaving home	76	53. Minor violation of the law	32
22. Gain of new family member other than child	75	54. Outstanding personal achievement	31
23. Religious intermarriage	71	55. Change in residence to better neighborhood	31
24. Breakup with boyfriend or girlfriend	67	56. Christmas	31
25. Mortgage over $10,000	66	57. Change in church activities	26
26. Change in residence to worse neighborhood	66	58. Change in number of family gatherings	24
27. Change in schools	66	59. Make move within city or area	23
28. Retirement	62	60. Change in recreation	23
29. Trouble with in-laws	60	61. Health of family member becomes better	21
30. Business readjustment	55	62. Change in residence to same type of neighborhood	13
31. Change to different line of work	54	63. Vacation	12
32. Revision of personal habits	53		

Interpretation: Divide your total score by half and interpret as with the Life Stress Scale I.

Student Stress Scale
Life Event Weights

	Age Groups		
Family Events	0-5	6-11	12-18
Death of a parent	106	109	108
Death of a sibling	75	86	88
Divorce of parents	68	73	70
Death of a grandparent	44	56	52
Ill parent (hospitalized)	49	52	52
Remarriage of parent	50	53	51
Birth of a sibling	50	50	50
Ill sibling (hospitalized)	43	47	49
Job loss by father	23	37	46
Decrease in parents' finances	21	29	43
Increase in parents' finances	20	28	41
New marital problem	38	44	41
Change in father's job	31	39	35
New adult in family	39	41	34
End of a marital problem	22	27	30
Mother beginning to work	42	40	28
Desirable Events			
End of a problem with parents	28	34	35
Recognition of achievement	12	21	24
Beginning nursery school, first grade, or high school	18	20	19
Receiving a special award	—	34	39
Being told you're attractive	—	23	26
Joining a church as an adult	—	21	25
Joining a social organization	—	15	18
Marriage	—	—	78
Beginning to date	—	—	42
Deciding to leave home	—	—	41
Getting your first permanent job	—	—	40
Being accepted at college	—	—	39
Getting a summer job	—	—	35
Finding a dating partner	—	—	34
Graduating from high school	—	—	33
Getting a driver's license	—	—	32
Stopping the use of drugs	—	—	30
Finding an adult friend	—	—	22

Undesirable Events

Death of a close friend	37	52	63
Illness of self (hospitalized)	50	53	50
New problem with parents	36	43	43
Change to a different school	25	35	41
Failing a grade in school	–	45	47
Becoming involved with drugs	–	38	45
Suspension from school	–	30	34
Failure in a desired activity	–	28	32
Being sent away from home	–	–	46
Breakup with boy/girlfriend	–	–	39
Involved in auto accident	–	–	36
Being told to break up	–	–	35
First appearance in juvenile court	–	–	31
Being invited to break the law	–	–	21

Copyright © R. Dean Coddington, M.D., 1979. Reprinted by permission. For more information on this Stress Scale as well as the Life Events Scale for Adolescents, contact Dr. Coddington at the Louisiana State University Medical Center, 1542 Tulane Avenue, New Orleans, Louisiana 70112.

Name _____ Date _____

School _____ District _____

Stress Profile for Teachers

Instructions

The Wilson Stress Profile for Teachers is designed to help you more clearly define, on a self-scoring basis, the areas and frequency of your stress. As you read each item, evaluate the statement in terms of a period of time rather than a specific day you remember. Indicate how often the source of stress occurs by circling the number that corresponds to the frequency of occurrence. Do not read the stress profile scoring sheet until after you have completed items 1-36.

	Never	Seldom	Sometimes	Often	Very Often

Student Behavior

1. I have difficulty controlling my class. 1 2 3 4 5
2. I become impatient/angry when my students do not
   do what I ask them to do 1 2 3 4 5
3. Lack of student motivation to learn affects
   the progress of my students negatively. 1 2 3 4 5
4. My students make my job stressful 1 2 3 4 5

                Total Items 1-4 _____

Employee/Administrator Relations

5. I have difficulty in my working relationship
   with my administrator(s) 1 2 3 4 5
6. My administrator makes demands of me that
   I cannot meet. 1 2 3 4 5
7. I feel I cannot be myself when I am interacting
   with my administrator 1 2 3 4 5
8. I feel my administrator does not approve of the job I do. 1 2 3 4 5

                Total Items 5-8 _____

Teacher/Teacher Relations

9. I feel isolated in my job (and its problems). 1 2 3 4 5
10. I feel my fellow teachers think I am not doing
    a good job 1 2 3 4 5
11. Disagreements with my fellow teachers are a
    problem for me. 1 2 3 4 5
12. I get too little support from the teachers with whom I work 1 2 3 4 5

                Total Items 9-12 _____

| | Never | Seldom | Sometimes | Often | Very Often |

Parent/Teacher Relations

13. Parents of my students are a source of concern for me 1 2 3 4 5
14. Parent's disinterest in their child's performance
    at school concerns me 1 2 3 4 5
15. I feel my students' parents think I am not doing
    a satisfactory job of teaching their children 1 2 3 4 5
16. The home environment of my students concerns me 1 2 3 4 5

                   Total Items 13-16 _____

Time Management

17. I have too much to do and not enough time to do it. 1 2 3 4 5
18. I have to take work home to complete it 1 2 3 4 5
19. I am unable to keep up with correcting papers
    and other school work 1 2 3 4 5
20. I have difficulty organizing my time in order to
    complete tasks 1 2 3 4 5

                   Total Items 17-20 _____

Intrapersonal Conflicts

21. I put self-imposed demands on myself to meet
    scheduled deadlines 1 2 3 4 5
22. I think badly of myself for not meeting
    the demands of my job 1 2 3 4 5
23. I am unable to express my stress to those who
    place demands on me 1 2 3 4 5
24. Teaching is stressful for me 1 2 3 4 5

                   Total Items 21-24 _____

Physical Symptoms of Stress

25. The frequency I experience one or more of these symptoms is:
    stomachaches, backaches, elevated blood pressure,
    stiff necks and shoulders 1 2 3 4 5
26. I find my job tires me out 1 2 3 4 5
27. I am tense by the end of the day 1 2 3 4 5
28. I experience headaches 1 2 3 4 5

                   Total Items 25-28 _____

Psychological/Emotional Symptoms of Stress

29. I find myself complaining to others 1 2 3 4 5
30. I am frustrated and/or feel angry 1 2 3 4 5
31. I worry about my job 1 2 3 4 5
32. I feel depressed about my job 1 2 3 4 5

                   Total Items 29-32 _____

Stress Management Techniques

| | Never | Seldom | Sometimes | Often | Very Often |

33. I am unable to use an effective method to manage my stress (such as exercise, relaxation techniques, etc.) 1 2 3 4 5
34. Stress management techniques would be useful in helping me cope with the demands of my job 1 2 3 4 5
35. I am now using one or more of the following to relieve my stress:
    alcohol, drugs, yelling, blaming, withdrawing, eating 1 2 3 4 5
36. I feel powerless to solve my difficulties 1 2 3 4 5

Total Items 33-36 _____

Scoring Sheet
Stress Profile for Teachers
Instructions for Scoring

1. After you have completed items 1-36, total the scores in each category and enter it in the corresponding box on this page.
2. Plot your score on the dotted line with an "X" and draw a line between your scoring "X's" so that a clear profile of your stress evaluation is visible.
3. Add up all your category scores and enter the number in the box after Total Overall Score. A score of 36-72 is low, 73-108 is moderate, and 109-180 is high.
4. Check your level on the same line as either low, moderate, or high.

Stress Profile Scores

Category	Score	Low (1-8)	Moderate (9-15)	High (16-20)
Student Behavior		· · · · · · · ·	· · · · · · ·	· · · · ·
Employee/Admin. Relations		· · · · · · · ·	· · · · · · ·	· · · · ·
Teacher/Teacher Relations		· · · · · · · ·	· · · · · · ·	· · · · ·
Parent/Teacher Relations		· · · · · · · ·	· · · · · · ·	· · · · ·
Time Management		· · · · · · · ·	· · · · · · ·	· · · · ·
Intrapersonal Conflicts		· · · · · · · ·	· · · · · · ·	· · · · ·
Physical Symptoms of Stress		· · · · · · · ·	· · · · · · ·	· · · · ·
Psych./Emotional Symp. of Stress		· · · · · · · ·	· · · · · · ·	· · · · ·
Stress Management Techniques		· · · · · · · ·	· · · · · · ·	· · · · ·

Total Overall Score [ ]   Low _____   Moderate _____   High _____
                              36-72   73-108   109-180

Copyright © 1979, Christopher F. Wilson. Reprinted by permission. All rights reserved.

"Hurry Sickness" Index

Please indicate how often each of the following applies to you in daily life.

		Never	Rarely	Sometimes	Often	Always
1.	Do you find yourself rushing your speech?	1	2	3	4	5
2.	Do you hurry other people's speech by interrupting them with "umhm, umhm" or by completing their sentences for them?	1	2	3	4	5
3.	Do you hate to wait in line?	1	2	3	4	5
4.	Do you seem to be short of time to get everything done?	1	2	3	4	5
5.	Do you detest wasting time?	1	2	3	4	5
6.	Do you eat too fast?	1	2	3	4	5
7.	Do you drive over the speed limit?	1	2	3	4	5
8.	Do you try to do more than one thing at a time?	1	2	3	4	5
9.	Do you become impatient if others do something too slowly?	1	2	3	4	5
10.	Do you seem to have little time to relax and enjoy the time of day?	1	2	3	4	5
11.	Do you find yourself overcommitted?	1	2	3	4	5
12.	Do you jiggle your knees or tap your fingers?	1	2	3	4	5
13.	Do you think about other things during conversations?	1	2	3	4	5
14.	Do you walk fast?	1	2	3	4	5
15.	Do you hate dawdling after a meal?	1	2	3	4	5
16.	Do you become irritable after a meal?	1	2	3	4	5
17.	Do you detest losing in sports or games?	1	2	3	4	5
18.	Do you find yourself with clenched fists or tight neck or jaw muscles?	1	2	3	4	5
19.	Does your concentration sometimes wander while you think about what's coming up later?	1	2	3	4	5
20.	Are you a competitive person?	1	2	3	4	5

Rule-of-Thumb Interpretation

20-60	O.K. (Possibly you're Type B)
61-79	Needs Improving
80+	Time Bomb!

Appendix B

Coping Scale

A number of ways people react to stress and tension are given below. Please indicate your own rating on each item by circling one of the five numbers at the right of each item. Please do not skip any items. You may take as much time as necessary. There are no right or wrong answers.

When I am feeling stress and tension:

		Never	Seldom	Sometimes	Usually	Always
1.	I use alcoholic beverages.	1	2	3	4	5
2.	I talk it out with others (friend, relative, or professional)	1	2	3	4	5
3.	I try to find out more about the situation	1	2	3	4	5
4.	I daydream.	1	2	3	4	5
5.	I believe in a supernatural power who cares about me.	1	2	3	4	5
6.	I work it off by physical exercise	1	2	3	4	5
7.	I try to see the humorous aspects of the situation	1	2	3	4	5
8.	I don't worry about it. Everything will probably work out fine.	1	2	3	4	5
9.	I sleep more	1	2	3	4	5
10.	I take some definite action on the basis of my present understanding	1	2	3	4	5
11.	I draw on my past experiences.	1	2	3	4	5
12.	I use food and food substitutes (smoking, chewing gum, eating more)	1	2	3	4	5
13.	I get prepared to expect the worst	1	2	3	4	5
14.	I curse.	1	2	3	4	5
15.	I make several alternate plans for handling the situation	1	2	3	4	5
16.	I use drugs.	1	2	3	4	5
17.	I become involved in other activities to keep my mind off the problem	1	2	3	4	5
18.	I cry.	1	2	3	4	5

Interpretation:

In general, the more long-term coping mechanisms you employ, the better, although sometimes a short-term mechanism is very useful and occasionally a long-term one is not useful. The items and their classification are:

1.	(Short-term)	10.	(Long-term)
2.	(Long-term)	11.	(Long-term)
3.	(Long-term)	12.	(Short-term)
4.	(Short-term)	13.	(Short-term)
5.	(Long-term)	14.	(Short-term)
6.	(Long-term)	15.	(Long-term)
7.	(Short-term)	16.	(Short-term)
8.	(Short-term)	17.	(Short-term)
9.	(Short-term)	18.	(Short-term)

Reproduced courtesy of Janice Bell. Adapted from Ms. Bell's master's thesis in Nursing, Loma Linda University.

The "Wellness Behavior" Test

This quiz will help you assess the behavior patterns that establish your own wellness. Use your judgment to give yourself a grade—A, B, C, D, or F, according to the following questions.

Relaxation:

1. Do you take time to get completely away from work and other pressures, to unwind?

Frequently	A
Fairly often	B
Sometimes	C
Seldom	D
I "just can't"	F

2. Do you sleep well? Fall asleep easily? Sleep through the night?

Very well	A
Fairly well	B
Not so well	C
Have trouble	D
"Certified Insomniac"	F

3. Do you take, or feel you need, aspirin, tranquilizers, sleeping pills, stomach medicines, or laxatives?

Seldom or never	A
Occasionally	B
Fairly often	C
Quite often	D
I'm hooked	F

4. Do you practice a form of deep relaxation (e.g., meditation, progressive relaxation, autogenic training, etc.) daily?

Nearly every day	A
Often	B
Occasionally	C
Seldom	D
What's deep relaxation?	F

Exercise:

1. Can you run a mile (at any speed) without becoming exhausted?

Easily	A
Fairly well	B
Can barely make it	C
Can't do it at all	D
Can't walk a mile	F

2. Can you play a fast game of tennis or other strenuous sport without becoming exhausted?

Easily	A
Fairly well	B
Get very tired	C
Get exhausted	D
Wouldn't try it	F

3. Do you jog or engage in some other very active exercise several times a week?

Usually	A
Fairly often	B
Occasionally	C
Seldom	D
Allergic to exercise	F

4. Are you fairly strong and physically able?

Very	A
Moderately	B
Adequate for my purposes	C
Quite weak	D
I can't stand up in a strong wind	F

Diet:

1. Are you overweight? (Just check to see how much surface fat is visible on your body.)

Not at all	A
Mildly overweight	B
Moderate amount of flab	C
Quite a paunch	D
Butterball	F

2. Do you smoke?

Never	A
2 or 3 a day	B
Half-pack a day	C
Pack or more a day	D
Chain smoker	F

3. Do you drink liquor (including wine or beer)?

Rarely or never	A
Socially and seldom	B
One a day	C
Several a day	D
I'm an alkie	F

4. Do you drink coffee, tea, cola drinks, or other sources of caffeine and sugar?

Rarely or never	A
1 or 2 a day	B
Several a day	C
Regularly, including with meals	D
Can't do without it	F

Interpretation: Assign 4 points for an A, 3 to a B, 2 to a C, and 1 to a D. Add up your points and divide by 12. How do you rate? A, "B+", or better means you're in good shape with three of the essential stress management ingredients. Anything less and you should be looking to change the area(s) of your weakness.

Copyright © 1979, Christopher F. Wilson. Reprinted by Permission.

Source: Albrecht, Karl. 1979. *Stress and the Manager.* Prentice-Hall. Reprinted by permission.

Appendix C

An Outside In Procedure for Relaxing

To begin this technique, find a comfortable chair to sit in. Let yourself settle in for a few minutes on each occasion before doing any of the exercises. The room the chair is in should be as quiet as possible and you should try to do these exercises around the same time each day. You will probably require about half an hour to start with, but as you become more adept, you will likely need only fifteen to twenty minutes.

Put the instructions onto a cassette tape. This will allow you to keep your eyes closed as you go through the various tension-release items. Be sure to talk in a smooth, rather monotone voice while recording it.

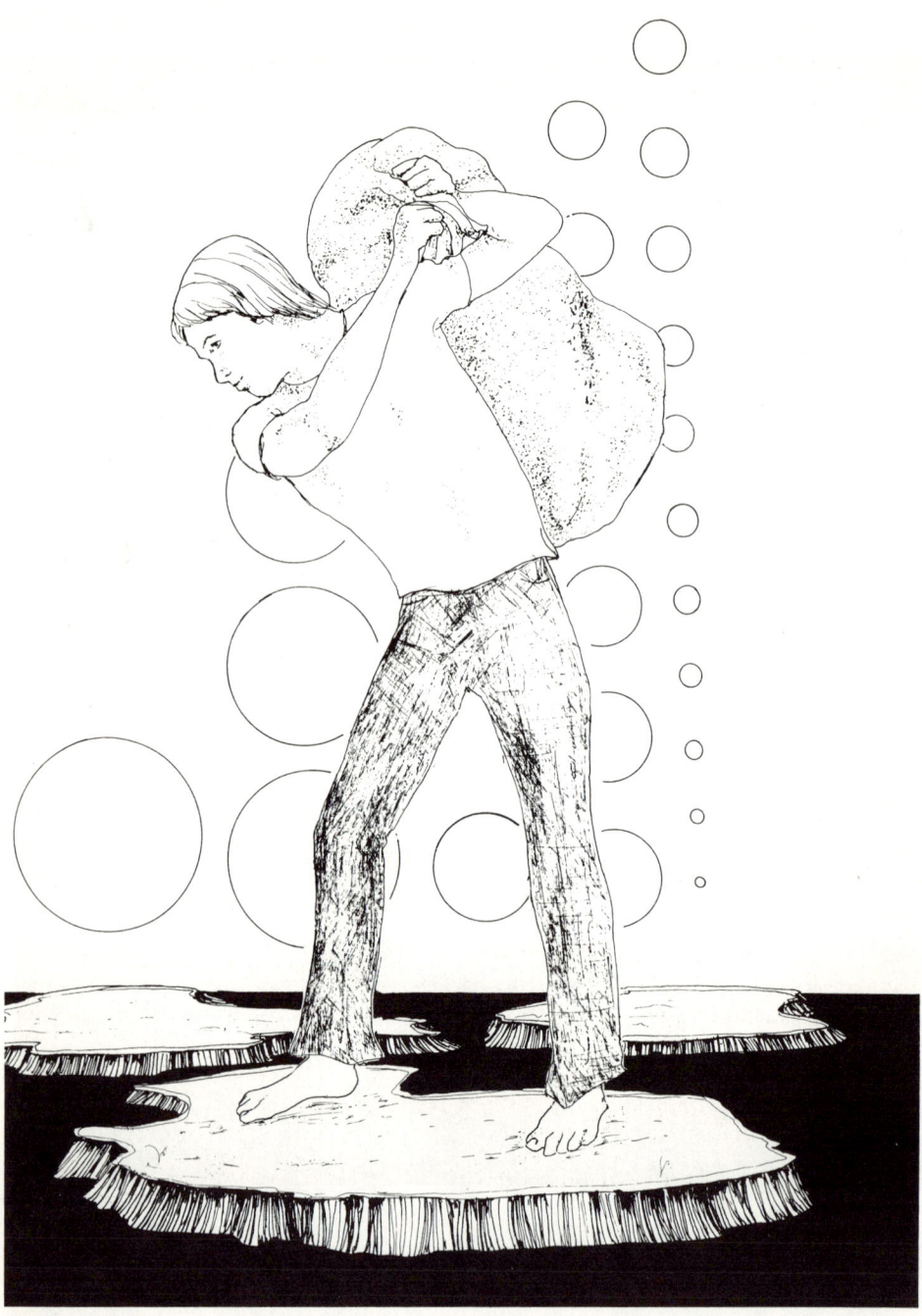

Instructions

Imagine yourself carrying all your responsibilities in a big sack on your shoulders. With your eyes closed, imagine yourself putting down your load. For this time of relaxation, you don't have to worry about anything. You are responsible for nothing. You don't have to do anything but relax.

As you relax your various muscle groups, you may also wish to use the following image. Think of a marionette standing up straight, being held up by taut strings that make it move. If the puppeteer's hands let go of the strings, they will go loose and the marionette will crumple into a totally relaxed heap. Your brain is your puppeteer and it can let go whenever it wants. As you relax each muscle, imagine letting go of the marionette strings, and as it goes limp, you go limp.

1. Now tighten your right hand by making a fist and squeezing (5 seconds). Notice the tension. Now let go. Imagine your limp puppet arm. Feel the difference (10 seconds). Now tighten your right arm again. Keep your eyes closed. Now let go. Feel the relaxation (10 seconds).

2. Now tighten your left arm (5 seconds). Now let go. Imagine your limp puppet arm. It should be as limp as your right limp puppet arm. Now squeeze again (5 seconds). Now let go. Feel the difference. Feel how relaxed both arms are. As they relax, notice how your torso and shoulders also relax.

3. Keep your eyes closed. Bring your shoulders up as if to touch your ears with them (5 seconds). Notice the tension. Now let go and feel the difference (10 seconds). Feel yourself letting go, going limp and loose and relaxed. Put down your bag of responsibilities. Just take it easy (15 seconds). Now bring your shoulders up again (5 seconds). Feel the tension. Now let go and notice the difference (10 seconds). Just take it easy. Keep your eyes closed. Notice how good you feel.

4. Now press your lips tightly together (5 seconds). Now let go and enjoy the difference (10 seconds). Try it again and let go once more, feeling the tension leave your mouth and jaw as you relax deeper and deeper.

5. Press your head back against your shoulders. Feel the tension in your neck (5 seconds). Now let go. Feel the difference (10 seconds). Keep your arms and torso relaxed, like the limp puppet. Now bring your head back again. Notice the tension. Now let go. Feel how good the relaxation feels. Keep your eyes closed.

6. Now take a deep breath—so deep you feel it stretch your chest muscles. Hold it (5 seconds). Release it slowly. Feel yourself relax and go limp as the air leaves your lungs. It's good. It feels very good. Now take a deep breath again. Feel the tension. Now relax and let the air out slowly. Now you feel your whole upper body is relaxed and limp and wonderful and that bag of cares seems so far away.

7. Now place your legs as far in front of you as you can. Now lift them slowly and hold (5 seconds). Feel the tension. Now let go and feel the difference (15 seconds). Feel the looseness that comes from letting go. Just hold it. Now lift your legs again and feel the tension. Now let go. Let your legs relax and become as loose and limp as your upper body. Feel the master puppeteer let go of more of the strings. Feel how good that feels.

8. Now point your toes back toward your chest. Feel the tension that creates in your calves. Now let go and experience the difference (10 seconds). Feel the relaxation. Now point your toes back again. See how tense your calves get. Now let go and see how good it feels to relax. To go limp and loose and easy.

9. Now curl your toes downward, like you're digging them into

sand. Feel the tension in your arches. Now let go. See how your feet are becoming as relaxed as the rest of your body. Now curl them again and feel the difference. Now let go. See how good it feels.

10. Now your whole body is relaxed. Notice how you feel and how good it is. Check over your body to see if any tension remains. If any part still feels somewhat tense, tighten it and then let go. Now you are like a balloon with the air all out, like a puppet with no strings attached. Feel the relaxation, the easiness. Enjoy the feeling. Enjoy how good it feels to have a few minutes with no responsibilities, no cares, just an easy relaxed feeling. Just a soothing tingle all over. Just a few minutes of the kind of break you deserve.

You could tape five to ten minutes of easy listening music at this point and let it play through as you enjoy the state of relaxation you have created.

After you are through, begin to straighten up in your chair. Give your body a chance to come back to its normal state of readiness. Stretch, take it easy, then open your eyes.

As you become more expert, you'll need to rely on the tape or written instructions less and less. You'll find you can relax this way without going through every muscle exercise. You may even find the images you have selected will "trigger" a pleasant twenty minutes or half-hour of relaxation.

Appendix D

An Outside In Procedure for Teaching Children to Relax

After you have prepared your students for the usefulness of relaxation procedures, you will want to begin a systematic procedure of relaxing with them. This outside in technique, adapted from an article in *Elementary School Guidance and Counseling* (October 1974) could be very useful to you. It follows the same sort of sequence as the adult technique in Appendix C but has images children can identify with easily.

Your students should be comfortably seated in their desks although, if your room is suitable, they can sit against the wall. Their backs should have a means of support.

Tell your students they must follow some rules. They must do exactly as you say. They must try each of the exercises. They should pay careful attention to how their muscles feel when they are tense and when they are relaxed. Finally, they must practice as you direct them (usually no more than twice daily).

Give some preliminary instructions about getting comfortably seated. Let both feet be on the floor and let their arms hang loosely by their sides. Have them close their eyes and not open them until instructed to do so by you. As mentioned in the text, if you have a student model the procedure, the process will go much more smoothly. You should now be ready to begin.

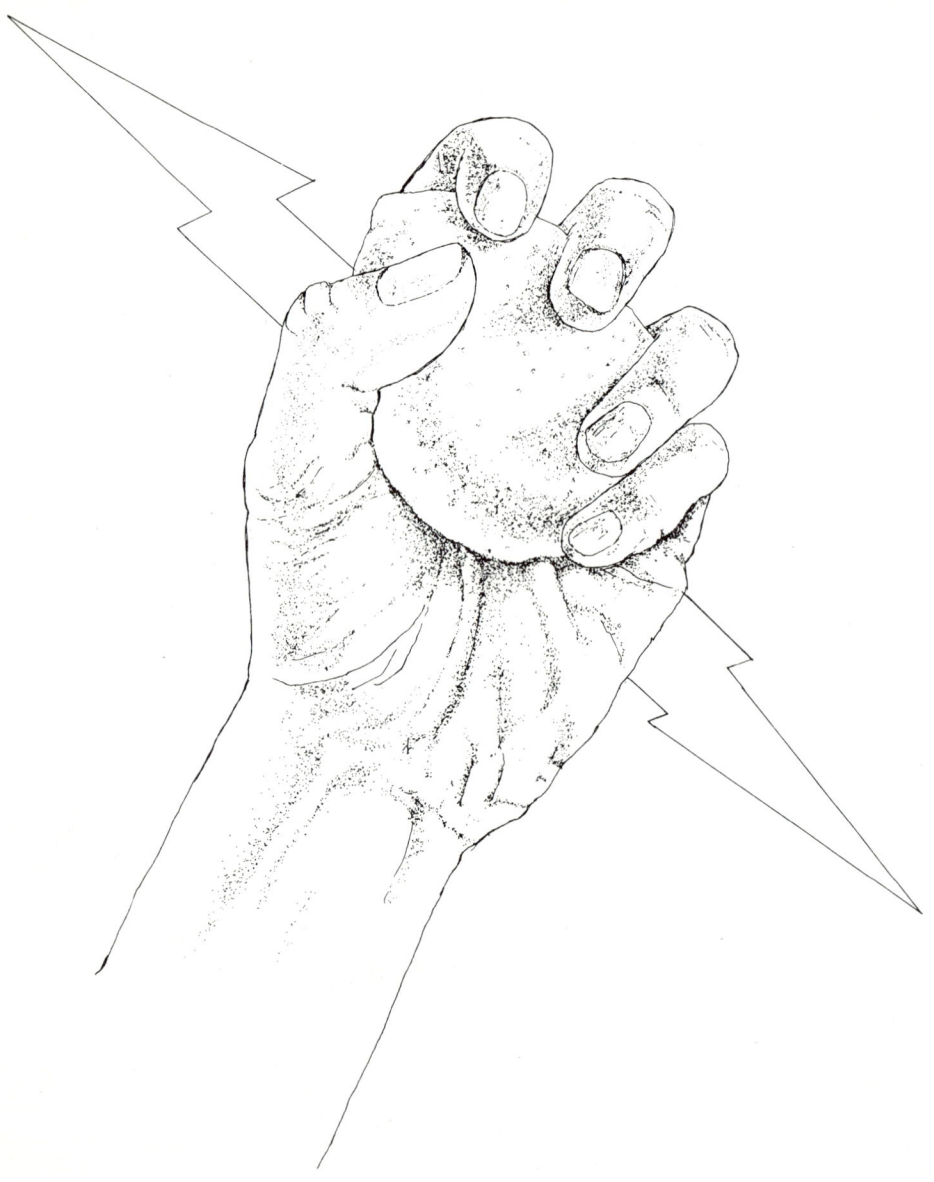

Hands and Arms

Pretend you have a whole lemon in your left hand. Squeeze it hard (5 seconds). Try to squeeze all the juice out. Feel how tight your hand and arm is as you squeeze. Now drop the lemon. Feel the difference (10 seconds). Take another lemon and squeeze it (5 seconds). Feel the tightness. Now drop the lemon and feel the relaxation.

Repeat the procedure for the right hand and arm.

Arms and Shoulders

    Pretend you are a furry, lazy cat. You really want to stretch. Stretch your arms in front of you. Raise them high over your shoulders. Feel the pull in your shoulders. Stretch higher (hold for 10-15 seconds). Now let your arms drop by your sides (10 seconds). Feel the difference. Stretch again. Put your arms way out in front of you. Raise them over your head. Pull them way back. Now let them drop quickly. Keep your eyes closed. Remember, you are a lazy cat and you are just yawning. You don't really want to wake up and see anything. Feel how good and warm and lazy it is to be relaxed.

Shoulder and Neck

Pretend you are a turtle. You're sitting on a rock by a very peaceful pond, just relaxing in the warm sun (15 seconds). Oh oh! You sense danger. Pull your head into your house. Try to pull your shoulders up to your ears and push your head down into your shoulders. Hold in tight (10 seconds). It isn't easy to be a turtle in a shell. The danger is past now. You can come out into the warm sunshine again. Once more, relax and feel the warm sun. Keep your eyes closed (15 seconds). Here it comes again! Pull your head back into your house and hold it tight (10 seconds). Protect yourself. Okay, you can come out again. Relax. Notice how much better it feels to be relaxed than to be all tightened up.

Face and Nose

Here comes a pesky fly. He has landed on your nose. Try to get him off without using your hands. Wrinkle up your nose. Make as many wrinkles in your nose as you can. Scrunch it up as hard as you can (10 seconds). Good. You chased him away. Now you can relax your nose. Feel how good it is without the fly (10 seconds). Oops, here he comes again. Right back in the middle of your nose. Shoo him away. Wrinkle up again. Hold it as tight as you can (10 seconds). Okay, he flew away. You can relax your face. Notice that when you scrunch up your nose that your cheeks and your mouth and your forehead and your eyes all help you and they get tight as well. When you relax your nose, the rest of your face relaxes too and that feels very good.

Stomach

Here comes a baby elephant. Oh-oh. He's not watching where he's going. He doesn't see you sitting there in the grass and he's about to step on your stomach. Don't move. You don't have time to get out of the way. Just get ready for him. Make your stomach very hard. Tighten up your stomach muscles. Hold it (10 seconds). It looks like he's going the other way. You can relax now. Let your stomach relax and be as soft as it can be (15 seconds). Feel how good that is. Oh-oh, he's coming back. Tighten up again. Real hard. If he steps on you it just won't hurt. Make your stomach like a rock. All right, he's moving away again. You can relax. Just get comfortable and feel relaxed in the warm sun in the open field.

At this point, you could let the students relax for a longer period of time, perhaps five minutes. It would be good to tape five minutes of music suitable for the purpose and let it play through at this point before you continue.

Legs and Feet

Pretend you are standing barefoot in a big mud puddle. Squish your toes down deep into the mud. Try to get your feet down to the bottom of the mud puddle. You'll probably need your legs to help you push. Push down, spread your toes apart, and feel the mud squish up between your toes. Now step up out of the mud puddle. Relax your feet (15 seconds). Let your toes go loose and feel how nice that is. Back into the mud puddle. Squish your toes down (10 seconds). Let your leg muscles help. Try to squeeze the puddle dry. Okay. Come back out now. Relax your feet, relax your legs. Relax your toes. It feels good to be relaxed, with no tension anywhere. Just warm and tingly.

Finishing

Stay as relaxed as you can. Let your whole body go limp and feel all your muscles relax. In a while, I will ask you to open your eyes and that will be the end of the session. As you go through the day, it is important to remember how good it feels to be relaxed. Sometimes you have to make yourself tighter before you can be relaxed, just like in today's exercises. You can practice these exercises at home. A good time is at night, after you have gone to bed and the lights are out and you won't be disturbed. It will help you get to sleep. When you become a good relaxer you can relax here at school. Just remember the elephant or the turtle or the mud puddle and you can do the exercises without anybody knowing.

Very slowly now, open your eyes and wiggle your muscles around a little. Very good. You've done a good job and will make super relaxers.

References

Chapter One

1. *Today's Education.* November/December 1979, p. 5.
2. Kyriacou, C. and Sutcliffe, J. 1978. Teacher stress: prevalence, sources, and symptoms. *British Journal of Educational Psychology* 48:159-167.
3. *Times Educational Supplement* (London), 1976. 3206:7.
4. *The Alberta Teacher's Association (ATA) Magazine,* March 1979, p. 2.
5. Wilson, C. 1979. Survey conducted in San Diego County. San Diego, California: Department of Education.
6. *The Toronto Star,* March 14, 1978.
7. Personal communication with the author.
8. Leroy Spaniel, Boston University.
9. Hendrickson, B. 1979. Teacher burnout: how to recognize it; what to do about it. *Learning,* January, pp. 36-39.
10. *Today's Education,* 1978, February/March, 67:1, p. 16 and *Today's Education,* 1979, February/March, 68:1, p. 20.
11. Bloch, A. 1977. The battered teacher. *Today's Education.* March/April. pp. 58-63.
12. Ibid., p. 58
13. Ibid., p. 59
14. Ibid., p. 59

15. Pickhardt, C., 1978. Fear in the schools: how students make teachers afraid. *Educational Leadership* 36:2.
16. Wells, R. 1978. Teacher survival in the classroom. *Journal of Research and Development in Education* 11:2, p. 72.
17. Howard, J., Cunningham, D., and Rechnitzer, P. 1978. *Rusting out, burning out, bowing out: stress and survival on the job.* Financial Post/MacMillan.
18. Wilson, C., op. cit.
19. Kyriacou, C. and Sutcliffe, J. op. cit.
20. Dunham, J. 1976. *Stress in schools.* Birmingham, England: National Association of Schoolmasters and Union of Teachers, p. 19.
21. Wilson, C., op. cit.

Chapter Two

1. Brenton, M. 1970. *What's happened to teacher?* New York: Coward, McCann, and Geoghegan.
2. Ibid., pp. 65-66.
3. Ibid., p. 69.
4. Ibid., p. 70.
5. Ibid.., p. 71.
6. Ibid., p. 69.
7. Ibid., p. 72.
8. Ibid., p. 74.

Chapter Three

1. *The Calgary Herald,* December 21, 1979, p. C12.
2. The class size/achievement issue: new evidence and a research plan. *Phi Delta Kappan,* March 1979.
3. More information may be obtained from Dr. Calvin Taylor, Bldg. No. 404, Dept. of Psychology, University of Utah, Salt Lake City, Utah 84112.

Chapter Four

1. Personal communication with the author.
2. Personal communication with the author.
3. Personal communication with the author.
4. *Education Unlimited.* 1979. November, 1:5, p. 37.
5. McDermott, J. F. 1976. Parental divorce in early childhood. In *Human adaptation.* Moos, R., ed., pp. 49-60. Lexington, Massachusetts: D. C. Heath.

6. Ibid., p. 55.
7. Ibid., p. 56.
8. Figures based on students in the province of Alberta, Canada. Informaation compiled by Dr. J. North, Regional Office of Education, Calgary, Alberta, Canada.
9. Department of Education, Province of Alberta, May 1979. Minister's Advisory Committee on Student Achievement (MACOSA) in the province of Alberta, Canada.
10. Ibid.
11. Holdaway, E. A. 1978. Teacher satisfaction: an Alberta report. Department of Educational Administration, the University of Alberta, Edmonton, Alberta, Canada.

Chapter Five

1. Hibbler, R. 1975. Life events and coping ability: a problem-solving approach. Dissertation Abstracts International. 36 (B), 4158. Columbus, Ohio: Ohio State University.
2. *Los Angeles Times,* December 6, 1979.
3. Rotter, J. B. 1966. General expectancies for internal versus external control of reinforcement. *Psychological Monographs* 80: Whole No. 609.
4. Rudd, W. G. A. and Wiseman, S. 1962. Sources of dissatisfaction among a group of teachers. *British Journal of Educational Psychology* 32: 275-291.
5. Holdaway, E. A., op. cit.
6. Maslow, A. 1954. *Motivation and personality.* New York: Harper and Row.
7. Ibid., p. 234.
8. Murray, E. 1972. Student's perception of self-actualizing and non-self-actualizing teachers. *The Journal of Teacher Education,* p. 385.

Chapter Six

1. Albrecht, K. 1979. *Stress and the manager: making it work for you.* Englewood Cliffs, New Jersey: Prentice-Hall.
2. Ibid., p. 11.
3. Toffler, A. 1970. *Future shock.* New York: Random House.
4. Albrecht, K., op. cit., p. 19.
5. Holmes, T. H. and Rahe, R. H. 1967. The social readjustment rating scale. *Journal of Psychosomatic Research* 11, p. 213.
6. Hough, R. L., Fairbank, D., and Garcia, A. 1976. *Journal of Health*

and Social Behavior 17:70-82.
7. Benson, H. 1975. *The relaxation response.* New York: William Morrow and Co.
8. Dean Coddington, M. D. Department of Psychiatry, Louisiana State University, School of Medicine. The scale also appeared in *Special Education Briefing,* October 1979. Waterford, Connecticut: Croft-Nei Publications.
9. Friedman, M. and Rosenman, R. 1974. *Type A behavior and your heart.* Greenwich, Connecticut: Fawcett Press.
10. Howard, Cunningham and Rechnitzer, op. cit.
11. Kostrubala, T. 1976. *The joy of running.* New York: Pocket Books.
12. Selye, H. 1974. *Stress without distress.* New York: Signet Books.
13. Ibid.
14. Levi, L. 1967. *Stress: sources, management and prevention.* New York: Liveright.
15. Wallace, R. K. and Benson, H. 1972. The physiology of meditation. *Scientific American* 226: 84-90.

Chapter Seven

1. Benson, H., op. cit.
2. Dudley, D. L. and Welke, E. 1977. *How to survive being alive.* New York: Doubleday.
3. Jacobson, E. 1938. *Progressive relaxation.* Chicago: The University of Chicago Press.
4. Ibid.
5. Wolpe, J. 1958. *Psychotherapy by reciprocal inhibition.* Stanford, California: Stanford University Press.
6. Benson, H., op. cit.
7. Truch, S. 1976. TM and teacher effectiveness. Department of Educational Psychology, The University of Calgary, Calgary, Alberta, Canada.
8. Howard, Cunningham and Rechnitzer, op. cit.
9. Kostrubala, op. cit.
10. Howard, Cunningham, and Rechnitzer, op. cit.
11. Kostrubala, op. cit.
12. Howard, Cunningham, and Rechnitzer, op. cit.
13. Janis, I. L. 1971. *Stress and frustration.* New York: Harcourt, Brace, Jovanovich.
14. Ibid.
15. Kyriacou, C. and Sutcliffe, J., op. cit.

16. Greden, J. F. 1974. Anxiety or caffeinism: a diagnostic dilemma. *American Journal of Psychiatry* 131:10, pp. 1089-1092.
17. U. S. Select Committee on National Nutrition. 1977. Washington, D.C.
18. Howard, Cunningham, and Rechnitzer, op. cit.

Chapter 8

1. Levent, B. and Gmelch, W. 1977. *Stress at the desk and how to creatively cope.* Oregon School Study Council Bulletin 21:4.
2. Ibid., p. 23.
3. Ibid., p. 28.
4. Huge, J., et al. 1973. School climate improvement: a challenge to the school administrator. *Phi Delta Kappan.*
5. Ibid., p. 83.
6. Ibid., p. 84.
7. Kyriacou, C. and Sutcliffe, J. 1979. Teacher stress and satisfaction. *Educational Research* 21:2, pp. 89-96.
8. Herzburg, F. 1966. *Work and the nature of man.* New York: T. Y. Crowell. See also *Learning* 9:3, June 1977.
9. Canadian Education Association Newsletter. May/June 1979.
10. Albrecht, K., op. cit.

Chapter Nine

1. Glassford, G. The values of participative physical education programs. Paper presented at the Trustee Effectiveness Workshop, Edmonton, January, 1980. Available from the Alberta School Trustees Association, 12310-105 Ave., Edmonton, Alberta, Canada.
2. Cautela, J. R. and Groden, J. 1978. *Relaxation: a comprehensive manual for adults, children and children with special needs.* Champaign, Illinois: Research Press.
3. Schneider, M. and Robin, A. *Turtle manual.* Stony Brook, New York: State University of New York.
4. *Gifted Child Quarterly,* Spring 1979, 23:1.
5. Uvaldo H. Palomares and G. Ball are the authors of the program. Information on the program can be obtained from: Human Development Training Institute, 7574 University Avenue, La Mesa, California 92041.
6. Conklin, R. C. 1976. Interpersonal skill training. *Australian Psychologist* 11:3, pp. 273-279. Further information can be obtained from Dr. Conklin at Foothills Educational Services Ltd., No. 306-4923-40 Avenue NW, Calgary, Alberta, Canada T3A 2N1.
   Also valuable is: *The heart of teaching series.* Agency for Instructional

Television, Box A, Bloomington, Indiana 47401. In Alberta or British Columbia, contact the Department of Education.
7. Meichenbaum, D. 1977. *Cognitive behavior modification.* New York: Plenum Press.
8. Glasser, W. 1969. *Schools without failure.* New York: Harper and Row.
9. Maranodola, P. and Imber, S. 1979. Glasser's classroom meeting: a humanistic approach to behavior change with pre-adolescent inner city learning disabled children. *Journal of Learning Disabilities* June/July, pp. 383-387.
10. Rowe, M. B. 1973. *Teaching science as continuous inquiry.* New York: McGraw-Hill.
11. Ibid.
12. Dr. Charles Glueck. Research conducted at the University of Cincinnati's Lipoprotein Research Laboratory.
13. Feingold, B. F. 1975. *Why your child is hyperactive.* New York: Random House.
14. Rapp, D. J. 1979. Food allergy treatment for hyperkinesis. *Journal of Learning Disabilities,* November 12:9, pp. 42-50.
15. Guilford, J. P. 1967. *The nature of human intelligence.* New York: McGraw-Hill.
16. Taylor, C. W. (ed.) 1978. *Teaching for talents and gifts: 1978 status.* U.S. Department of Health, Education and Welfare, pp. 20-37.
17. Ibid.
18. Taylor, C. W., op. cit., p. xii.
19. Taylor, C. W. Department of Psychology, University of Utah, Salt Lake City, Utah 84112.
20. Taylor, C. W., op. cit., p. x.

About the Author

Stephen Truch, PhD, is currently a consulting psychologist in Calgary, Alberta. He was a teacher for several years prior to entering graduate school. After completing his PhD from the University of Calgary, he became Assistant Superintendent for Special Education with the County of Mountain View.

He has had a ten year interest in the area of stress and its implications for education. Dr. Truch has spoken to many audiences and conducted numerous seminars and workshops on creative stress management throughout Canada and the United States. He served for two years on the Board of Directors of the Calgary Association for Learning Disabilities.

He is married and has two daughters.